James Allen on Prosperity and Success

by James Allen

James Allen on Prosperity and Success

Eight Pillars of Prosperity
Foundation Stones to Happiness and Success
The Path to Prosperity

Eight Pillars of Prosperity

Table of Contents

Preface

It is popularly supposed that a greater prosperity for individuals or nations can only come through a political and social reconstruction. This cannot be true apart from the practice of the moral virtues in the individuals that comprise a nation. Better laws and social conditions will always follow a higher realisation of morality among the individuals of a community, but no legal enactment can give prosperity to, nay it cannot prevent the ruin of, a man or a nation that has become lax and decadent in the pursuit and practice of virtue.

The moral virtues are the foundation and support of prosperity as they are the soul of greatness. They endure for ever, and all the works of man which endure are built upon them. Without them there is neither strength, stability, nor substantial reality, but only ephemeral dreams. To find moral principles is to have found prosperity, greatness, truth, and is therefore to be strong, valiant, joyful and free.

James Allen

Eight Pillars

Prosperity rests upon a moral foundation. It is popularly supposed to rest upon an immoral foundation — that is, upon trickery, sharp practice, deception and greed. One commonly hears even an otherwise intelligent man declare that "No man can be successful in business unless he is dishonest," thus regarding business prosperity – a good thing – as the effect of dishonesty – a bad thing. Such a statement is superficial and thoughtless, and reveals a total lack of knowledge of moral causation, as well as a very limited grasp of the facts of life. It is as though one should sow henbane and reap spinach, or erect a brick house on a quagmire — things impossible in the natural order of causation, and therefore not to be attempted. The spiritual or moral order of causation is not different in principle, but only in nature. The same law obtains in things unseen – in thoughts and deeds — as in things seen – in natural phenomena. Man sees the processes in natural objects, and acts in accordance with them, but not seeing the spiritual processes, he imagines that they do not obtain, and so he does not act in harmony with them.

Yet these spiritual processes are just as simple and just as sure as the natural processes. They are indeed the same natural modes manifesting in the world of mind. All the parables and a large number of the sayings of the Great Teachers are designed to illustrate this fact. The natural world is the mental world made visible. The seen is the mirror of the unseen. The upper half of a circle is in no way different from the lower half, but its sphericity is reversed. The material and the mental are not two detached arcs in the universe, they are the two halves of a complete circle. The natural and the spiritual are not at eternal enmity, but in the true order of the universe are eternally at one. It is in the unnatural — in the abuse of function and faculty – where division arises, and where main is wrested back, with repeated sufferings, from the perfect circle from which he has tried to depart. Every process in matter is also a process in mind. Every natural law has its spiritual counterpart.

Take any natural object, and you will find its fundamental processes in the mental sphere if you rightly search. Consider, for instance, the germination of a seed and its growth into a plant with the final development of a flower, and back to seed again. This also is a mental process. Thoughts are seeds which, falling in the soil of the mind, germinate and develop until they reach the completed stage, blossoming into deeds good or bad, brilliant or stupid, according to their nature, and ending as seeds of thought to be again sown in other minds. A teacher is a sower of seed, a spiritual agriculturist, while he who teaches himself is the wise farmer of his own mental plot. The growth of a thought is as the growth of a plant. The seed must be sown seasonably, and time is required for its full development into the plant of knowledge and the flower of wisdom.

While writing this, I pause, and turn to look through my study window, and there, a hundred yards away, is a tall tree in the top of which some enterprising rook from a rookery hard by, has, for the first time, built its nest. A strong, north-east wind is blowing, so that the top of the tree is swayed violently to and fro by the onset of the blast; yet there is no danger to that frail thing of sticks and hair, and the mother bird, sitting upon her eggs, has no fear of the storm. Why is this? It is because the bird has instinctively built her nest in harmony with principles which ensure the maximum strength and security. First, a fork is chosen as the foundation for the nest, and not a space between two separate branches, so that, however great may be the swaying of the tree top, the position of the nest is not altered, nor its structure disturbed; then the nest is built on a circular plan so as to offer the greatest resistance to any external pressure, as well as to obtain more perfect compactness within, in accordance with its purpose; and so, however the tempest may rage, the birds rest in comfort and security. This is a very simple and familiar object, and yet, in the strict obedience of its structure to mathematical law, it becomes, to the wise, a parable of enlightenment, teaching them that only by ordering one's deeds in accordance with fixed principles is perfect surety, perfect security, and perfect peace obtained amid the uncertainty of events and the turbulent tempests of life.

A house or a temple built by man is a much more complicated structure than a bird's nest, yet it is erected in accordance with those mathematical principles which are everywhere evidenced in nature. And here is seen how man, in material things, obeys universal principles. He never attempts to put up a building in defiance of geometrical proportions, for he knows that such a building would be unsafe, and that the first storm would, in all probability, level it to the ground, if, indeed, it did not fall about his ears during the process of erection. Man in his material building scrupulously obeys the fixed principles of circle, square and angle, and, aided by rule, plumbline, and compasses, he raises a structure which will resist the fiercest storms, and afford him a secure shelter and safe protection.

All this is very simple, the reader may say. Yes, it is simple because it is true and perfect; so true that it cannot admit the smallest compromise, and so perfect that no man can improve upon it. Man, through long experience, has learned these principles of the material world, and sees the wisdom of obeying them, and I have thus referred to them in order to lead up to a consideration of those fixed principles in the mental or spiritual world which are just as simple, and just as eternally true and perfect, yet are at present so little understood by man that he daily violates them, because ignorant of their nature, and unconscious of the harm he is all the time inflicting upon himself.

In mind as in matter, in thoughts as in things, in deeds as in natural processes, there is a fixed foundation of law which, if consciously or ignorantly ignored leads to disaster, and defeat. It is, indeed, the ignorant violation of this law which is the cause of the world's pain and sorrow. In matter, this law is presented as mathematical; in mind, it is perceived as moral. But the mathematical and the moral are not separate and opposed; they are but two aspects of a united whole. The fixed principles of mathematics, to which all matter is subject, are the body of which the spirit is ethical; while the eternal principles of morality are mathematical truisms operating in the universe of mind. It is as impossible to live successfully apart from moral principles, as to build successfully while ignoring mathematical principles. Characters, like houses, only stand firmly when built on a foundation of moral law — and they are built up slowly and laboriously, deed by deed, for in the building of character, the bricks are deeds. Business and all human enterprises are not exempt from the eternal order, but can only stand securely by the observance of fixed laws. Prosperity, to be stable and enduring, must rest on a solid foundation of moral principle, and be supported by the adamantine pillars of sterling character and moral worth. In the attempt to run a business in defiance of moral principles, disaster, of one kind or another, is inevitable. The permanently prosperous men in any community are not its tricksters and deceivers, but its reliable and upright men. The Quakers are acknowledged to be the most upright men in the British community, and, although their numbers are small, they are the most prosperous. The Jains in India are similar both in numbers and sterling worth, and they are the most prosperous people in India.

Men speak of "building up a business," and, indeed, a business is as much a building as is a brick house or a stone church, albeit the process of building is a mental one. Prosperity, like a house, is a roof over a man's head, affording him protection and comfort. A roof presupposes a support, and a support necessitates a foundation. The roof of prosperity, then, is supported by the following eight pillars which are cemented in a foundation of moral consistency:—

1. Energy
2. Economy
3. Integrity
4. System
5. Sympathy
6. Sincerity
7. Impartiality
8. Self-reliance

A business built up on the faultless practice of all these principles would be so firm and enduring as to be invincible. Nothing could injure it; nothing could undermine its prosperity, nothing could interrupt its success, or bring it to the ground; but that success would be assured with incessant increase so long as the principles were adhered to. On the other hand, where these principles were all absent, there could be no success of any kind; there could not even be a business at all, for there would be nothing to produce the adherence of one part with another; but there would be that lack of life, that absence of fibre and consistency which animates and gives body and form to anything whatsoever. Picture a man with all these principles absent from his mind, his daily life, and even if your knowledge of these principles is but slight and imperfect, yet you could not think of such a man as doing any successful work. You could picture him as leading the confused life of a shiftless tramp but to imagine him at the head of a business, as the centre of an organisation, or as a responsible and controlling agent in any department of life – this you could not do, because you realise its impossibility. The fact that no one of moderate morality and intelligence can think of such a man as commanding any success, should, to all those who have not yet grasped the import of these principles, and therefore declare that morality is not a factor, but rather a hindrance, in prosperity, be a sound proof to them that their conclusion is totally wrong, for if it was right, then the greater the lack of these moral principles, the greater would be the success.

These eight principles, then, in greater or lesser degree, are the causative factors in all success of whatsoever kind. Underneath all prosperity they are the strong supports, and, howsoever appearances may be against such a conclusion, a measure of them informs and sustains every effort which is crowned with that excellence which men name success.

It is true that comparatively few successful men practice, in their entirety and perfection, all these eight principles, but there are those who do, and they are the leaders, teachers, and guides of men, the supports of human society, and the strong pioneers in the van of human evolution.

But while few achieve that moral perfection which ensures the acme of success, all lesser successes come from the partial observance of these principles which are so powerful in the production of good results that even perfection in any two or three of them alone is sufficient to ensure an ordinary degree of prosperity, and maintain a measure of local influence at least for a time, while the same perfection in two or three with partial excellence in all, or nearly all, the others, will render permanent that limited success and influence which will, necessarily, grow and extend in exact ratio with a more intimate knowledge and practice of those principles which, at present, are only partially incorporated in the character.

The boundary lines of a man's morality mark the limits of his success. So true is this that to know a man's moral status would be to know – to mathematically gauge – his ultimate success or failure. The temple of prosperity only stands in so far as it is supported by its moral pillars; as they are weakened, it becomes insecure; in so far as they are withdrawn, it crumbles away and totters to ruin.

Ultimate failure and defeat are inevitable where moral principles are ignored or defied – inevitable in the nature of things as cause and effect. As a stone thrown upward returns to the earth, so every deed, good or bad, returns upon him that sent it forth. Every unmoral or immoral act frustrates the end at which it aims, and every such succeeding act puts it further and further away as an achieved realisation. On the other hand, every moral act is another solid brick in the temple of prosperity, another round of strength and sculptured beauty in the pillars which support it.

Individuals, families, nations grow and prosper in harmony with their growth in moral strength and knowledge; they fall and fail in accordance with their moral decadence.

Mentally, as physically, only that which has form and solidity can stand and endure. The unmoral is nothingness, and from it nothing can be formed. It is the negation of substance. The immoral is destruction. It is the negation of form. It is a process of spiritual denudation. While it undermines and disintegrates, it leaves the scattered material ready for the wise builder to put it into form again; and the wise builder is Morality. The moral is substance, form, and building power in one. Morality always builds up and preserves, for that is its nature, being the opposite of immorality, which always breaks down and destroys. Morality is the master–builder everywhere, whether in individuals or nations.

Morality is invincible, and he who stands upon it to the end, stands upon an impregnable rock, so that his defeat is impossible, his triumph certain. He will be tried, and that to the uttermost, for without fighting there can be no victory, and so only can his moral powers be perfected, and it is in the nature of fixed principles, as of everything finely and perfectly wrought, to have their strength tested and proved. The steel bars which are to perform the strongest and best uses in the world must be subjected to a severe strain by the ironmaster, as a test of their texture and efficiency, before they are sent from his foundry. The brickmaker throws aside the bricks which have given way under the severe heat. So he who is to be greatly and permanently successful will pass through the strain of adverse circumstances and the fire of temptation with his moral nature not merely not undermined, but strengthened and beautified. He will be like a bar of well-wrought steel, fit for the highest use, and the universe will see, as the ironmaster his finely-wrought steel, that the use does not escape him.

Immorality is assailable at every point, and he who tries to stand upon it, sinks into the morass of desolation. Even while his efforts seem to stand, they are crumbling away. The climax of failure is inevitable. While the immoral man is chuckling over his ill-gotten gains, there is already a hole in his pocket through which his gold is falling. While he who begins with morality, yet deserts it for gain in the hour of trial, is like the brick which breaks on the first application of heat; he is not fit for use, and the universe casts him aside, yet not finally, for he is a being, and not a brick; and he can live and learn, can repent and be restored.

Moral force is the life of all success, and the sustaining element in all prosperity; but there are various kinds of success, and it is frequently necessary that a man should fail in one direction that he may reach up to a greater and more far-reaching success. If, for instance, a literary, artistic, or spiritual genius should begin by trying to make money, it may be, and often is, to his advantage and the betterment of his genius that he should fail therein, so that he may achieve that more sublime success wherein lies his real power. Many a millionaire would doubtless be willing to barter his millions for the literary success of a Shakespeare or the spiritual success of a Buddha, and would thereby consider that he had made a good bargain. Exceptional spiritual success is rarely accompanied with riches, yet financial success cannot in any way compare with it in greatness and grandeur. But I am not, in this book, dealing with the success of the saint or spiritual genius but with that success which concerns the welfare, well-being, and happiness of the broadly average man and woman, in a word, with the prosperity which, while being more or less connected with money – being present and temporal – yet is not confined thereto, but extends to and embraces all human activities, and which particularly relates to that harmony of the individual with his circumstances which produces that satisfaction called happiness and that comfort known as prosperity. To the achievement of this end, so desirable to the mass of mankind, let us now see how the eight principles operate, how the roof of prosperity is raised and made secure upon the pillars by which it is supported.

First Pillar – Energy

Energy is the working power in all achievement. Inert coal it converts into fire, and water it transmutes into steam; it vivifies and intensifies the commonest talent until it approaches to genius, and when it touches the mind of the dullard, it turns into a living fire that which before was sleeping in inertia.

Energy is a moral virtue, its opposing vice being laziness. As a virtue, it can be cultivated, and the lazy man can become energetic by forcibly arousing himself to exertion. Compared with the energetic man, the lazy man is not half alive. Even while the latter is talking about the difficult of doing a thing, the former is doing it. the active man has done a considerable amount of work before the lazy man has roused himself from sleep. While the lazy man is waiting for an opportunity, the active man has gone out, and met and utilized half a dozen opportunities. He does things while the other is rubbing his eyes.

Energy is one of the primary forces: without it nothing can be accomplished. It is the basic element in all forms of action. The entire universe is a manifestation of tireless, though inscrutable energy. Energy is, indeed, life, and without it there would be no universe, no life. When a man has ceased to act, when the body lies inert, and all the functions have ceased to act, then we say he is dead; and in so far as a man fails to act, he is so far dead. Man, mentally and physically, is framed for action, and not for swinish ease. Every muscle of the body (being a lever for exertion) is a rebuke to the lazy man. Every bone and nerve is fashioned for resistance; every function and faculty is there for a legitimate use. All things have their end in action; al things are perfected in use.

This being so, there is no prosperity for the lazy man, no happiness, no refuge and no rest; for him, there is not even the ease which he covets, for he at last becomes a homeless outcast, a troubled, harried, despised man, so that the proverb wisely puts it that "The lazy man does the hardest work," in that, avoiding the systematic labour of skill, he brings upon himself the hardest lot.

Yet energy misapplied is better than no energy at all. This is powerfully put by St. John in the words: "I would have you either hot or cold; if you are lukewarm I will spew you out of my mouth." The extremes of heat and cold here symbolize the transforming agency of energy, in its good and bad aspects.

The lukewarm stage is colourless, lifeless, useless; it can scarcely be said to have either virtue or vice, and is merely barren empty, fruitless. The man who applies his abounding energy to bad ends, has, at the very power with which the strives to acquire his selfish ends, will bring upon him such difficulties, pains, and sorrows, that will compel him to learn by experience, and so at last to re-fashion his base of action. At the right moment, when his mental eyes open to better purposes, he will turn round and cut new and proper channels for the outflow of his power, and will then be just as strong in good as he formerly was in evil. This truth is beautifully crystallized in the old proverb, "The greater the sinner, the great the saint."

Energy is power, and without it there will be no accomplishment; there will not even be virtue, for virtue does not only consist of not doing evil, but also, primarily, of doing good. There are those who try, yet fail through insufficient energy. Their efforts are too feeble to produce positive results. Such are not vicious, and because they never do any deliberate harm, are usually spoken of as good men that fail. But to lack the initiative to do harm is not to be good; it is only to be weak and powerless. He is the truly good man who, having the power to do evil, yet chooses to direct his energies in ways that are good. Without a considerable degree of energy, therefore, there will be no moral power. What good there is, will be latent and sleeping; there will be no going forth of good, just as there can be no mechanical motion without the motive power.

Energy is the informing power in all doing in every department of life, and whether it be along material or spiritual lines. The call to action, which comes not only from the soldier but from the lips or pen of every teacher in every grade of thought, is a call to men to rouse their sleeping energy, and to do vigorously the task in hand. Even the men of contemplation and mediation never cease to rouse their disciples to exertion in meditative thought, is a call to men to rouse their sleeping energy, and to do vigorously the task in hand. Even the men of contemplation and meditation never cease to rouse their disciples to exertion in meditative thought. Energy is alike needed in all spheres of life, and not only are the rules of the soldier, the engineer and the merchant rules of action, but nearly all the percepts of the saviors, sages, and saints are precepts of doing.

The advice of one of the Great Teachers to his disciples – "Keep wide awake," tersely expresses the necessity for tireless energy if one's purpose is to be accomplished, and is equally good advice to the salesman as to the saint. "Eternal vigilance is the price of liberty," and liberty is the reaching of one's fixed end. It was the same Teacher that said: "If anything is to be done, let a man do it at once; let him attack it vigorously!" The wisdom of this advice is seen when it is remembered that action is creative, that increase and development follow upon legitimate use. To get more energy we must use to the full that which we already possess. Only to him that that is given. Only to him that puts his hand vigorously to some task does power and freedom come.

But energy, to be productive, must not only be directed towards good ends, it must be carefully controlled and conserved. "The conservation of energy" is a modern term expressive of that principle in nature by which no energy is wasted or lost, and the man whose energies are to be fruitful in results must work intelligently upon this principle. Noise and hurry are so much energy running to waste. "More haste, less speed." The maximum of noise usually accompanies the minimum of accomplishment. With much talk there is little doing. Working steam is not heard. It is the escaping steam which makes a great noise. It is the concentrated powder which drives the bullet to its mark.

In so far as a man intensifies his energies by conserving them, and concentrating them upon the accomplishment of his purpose, just so far does he gain quietness and silence, in response and calmness. It is great delusion that noise means power. There is no great baby than the blustering boaster. Physically a man, he is but an infant mentally, and having no strength to anything, and no work to show, he tries to make up for it by loudly proclaiming what he has done, or could do.

"Still waters run deep," and the great universal forces are inaudible. Where calmness is, there is the greatest power. Calmness is the sure indication of a strong, welltrained, patiently disciplined mind. The calm man knows his business, be sure of it. His words are few, but they tell. His schemes are well planned, and they work true, like a well balanced machine. He sees a long way ahead, and makes straight for his object. The enemy, Difficulty, he converts into a friend, and makes profitable use of him, for he has studied well how to "agree with his adversary while he is in the way with him," Like a wise general, he has anticipated all emergencies. Indeed, he is the man who is prepared beforehand. In his meditations, in the counsels of his judgement, he has conferred with causes, and has caught the bent of all contingencies. He is never taken by surprise; is never in a hurry, is safe in the keeping of his own steadfastness, and is sure of his ground. You may think you have got him, only to find, the next moment, that you have tripped in your haste, and that he has got you, or rather that you, wanting calmness, have hurried yourself into the dilemma which you had prepared for him. Your impulse cannot do battle with his deliberation, but is foiled at the first attack; your uncurbed energy cannot turn aside the wisely directed steam of his concentrated power. He is "armed at all points." By a mental Ju-Jitsu acquired through self discipline, he meets opposition in such a way that it destroys itself. Upbraid him with angry words, and the reproof hidden in his gentle reply searches to the very heart of your folly, and the fire of your anger sinks into the ashes of remorse. Approach him with a vulgar familiarity, and his look at once fill you with shame, and brings you back to your senses. As he is prepared for all events, so he is ready for all men; though no men are ready for him. All weaknesses are betrayed in his presence, and he commands by an inherent force which calmness has rendered habitual and unconscious.

Calmness, as distinguished from the dead placidity of languor, is the acme of concentrated energy. There is a focused mentality behind it. in agitation and excitement the mentality is dispersed. It is irresponsible, and is without force or weight. The fussy, peevish, irritable man has no influence. He repels, and not attracts. He wonders why his "easy going" neighbour succeeds, and is sought after, while he, who is always hurrying, worrying and troubling the miscalls it striving, falls and is avoided. His neighbour, being a calmer man, not more easy going but more deliberate, gets through more work, does it more skillfully, and is more self possessed and manly. This is the reason of his success and influence. His energy is controlled and used, while the other man's energy is dispersed and abused.

Energy, then, is the first pillar in the temple of prosperity, and without it, as the first and most essential equipment, there can be no prosperity. No energy means no capacity; there is no manly self respect and independence. Amongst the unemployed will be found many who are unemployable through sheer lack of this first essential of work energy. The man that stands many hours a day at a street corner with his hands in his pockets and a pipe in his mouth, waiting for some one to treat him to a glass of beer, is little likely to find employment, or to accept it should it come to him. Physically flabby and mentally inert, he is every day becoming more some, is making himself more unfit to work, and therefore unfit to live. The energetic man may pass through temporary periods of unemployment and suffering, but it is impossible for him to become one of the permanently unemployed. He will either find work or make it, for inertia is painful to him, and work is a delight; and he who delights in work will not long remain unemployed.

The lazy man does not wish to be employed. He is in his element when doing nothing. His chief study is how to avoid exertion. To vegetate in semi torpor is his idea of happiness. He is unfit and unemployable. Even the extreme Socialist, who places all unemployment, at the door of the rich, would discharge a lazy, neglectful and unprofitable servant, and so add one more to the arm of the unemployed; for laziness is one of the lowest vices repulsive to all active, right minded men.

But energy is a composite power. It does not stand alone. Involved in it are qualities which go to the making of vigorous character and the production of prosperity. Mainly, these qualities are contained in the four following characteristics:—

1. Promptitude
2. Vigilance
3. Industry
4. Earnestness

The pillar of energy is therefore a concrete mass composed of these four tenacious elements. They are through, enduring, and are calculated to withstanding the wildest weather of adversity. They all make for life, power, capacity, and progress.

Promptitude is valuable possession. It begets reliability. People who are alert, prompt, and punctual are relied upon. They can be trusted to do their duty, and to do it vigorously and well. Masters who are prompt are a tonic to their employees, and a whip to those who are inclined to shirk. They are a means of wholesome discipline to those who would not otherwise discipline themselves. Thus while aiding their own usefulness and success, they contribute to the usefulness and success of others. The perfunctory worker, who is ever procrastinating, and is always behind time, becomes a nuisance, if not go himself, to others, and his services come to be regarded as of little economic value. Deliberation and dispatch, handmaids of promptitude, are valuable aids in the achievement of prosperity. In ordinary business channels, alacrity is a saving power, and promptness spells profit. It is doubtful whether a confirmed procrastinator ever succeeded in business. I have not yet met one such, though I have known many who have failed.

Vigilance is the guard of all the faculties and powers of the mind. It is the detective that prevents the entrance of any violent and destructive element. It is the close companion and protector of all success, liberty, and wisdom. Without this watchful attitude of mind, a man is a fool, and there is no prosperity for a fool. The fool allows his mind to be ransacked and robbed of its gravity, serenity, and judgement by mean thoughts and violent passions as they come along to molest him. He is never on his guard, but leaves open the doors of his mind to every nefarious intruder. He is so weak and unsteady as to be swept off his balance by every gust of impulse that overtakes him. He is an example to others of what they should not be. He is always a failure, for the fool is an offence to all men, and there is no society that can receive him with respect. As wisdom is the acme of strength, so folly is the other extreme of weakness.

The lack of vigilance is shown in thoughtlessness and in a general looseness in the common details of life. Thoughtlessness is built another name for folly. It lies at the root of a great deal of failure and misery. No one who aims at any kind of usefulness and prosperity (for usefulness in the body politic and prosperity to one's self cannot be served)' can afford to be asleep with regard to his actions and the effect of those actions on other and reactively on himself. He must, at the outset of his career, wake up to a sense of his personnel responsibility. He must know that wherever he is – in the home, the counting — house, the pulpit, the store, in the schoolroom or behind the counter, in company or alone, at work or at play — his conduct will materially affect his career for good or bad; for there is a subtle influence in behavior which leaves its impression every man, woman, and child that it touches, and that impress is the determining factor in the attitude of persons towards one another. It is for the reason that the cultivation of good manners plays such an important part in all coherent society. If you carry about with you a disturbing or disagreeable mental defect, it needs not to be named and known to work its poison upon your affairs. Its corrosive influence will eat into all your efforts, and disfigure your happiness and prosperity, as powerful acid eats into and disfigures the finest steel. On the other hand, if you carry about an assuring and harmonious mental excellence, it needs no that those about you understand it to be influenced by it. They will be drawn towards you in good –will, often without knowing why, and that good quality will be the most powerful sport in all your affairs, bringing you friends and opportunities, and greatly aiding in the success of all your enterprises. It will even right your minor incapacitaties; covering a multitude of faults.

Thus we receive at the hands of the world according to the measure of our giving. For bad, bad; for good, good. For defective conduct, indifferent influence and imperfect success; for superior conduct lasting power and consummate achievement. We act, and the world responds. When the foolish man fails, he blames other, and sees no error in himself; but the wise man watches and corrects himself, and so is assured of success.

The man whose mind is vigilant and alert, has thereby a valuable equipment in the achievement of his aims; and if he be fully alive and wide-awake on all occasions, to all opportunities, and against all marring defects of character, what event, what circumstance, what enemy shall overtake him and find him unprepared? What shall prevent him from achieving the legitimate and at which he aims?

Industry brings cheerfulness and plenty. Vigorously industrious people are the happiest members of the community. They are not always the richest, if by riches is meant a superfluity of money; but they are always the most lighthearted and joyful, and the most satisfied with what they do and have, and are therefore the richer, if by richer we mean more abundantly blessed. Active people have no time for moping and brooding, or for dwelling selfishly upon their ailments and troubles. Things most used are kept the brightest, and people most employed best retain their brightness and buoyancy of spirit. Things unused tarnish quickest; and the time killer is attacked with ennui and morbid fancies. To talk of having to "kill time" is almost like a confession of imbecility; for who, in the short life at his disposal, and in a world so flooded with resources of knowledge with sound heads and good hearts can fill up every moment of every day usefully and happily, and if they refer to time at all, it is to the effect that it is all too short to enable them to do all that they would like to do.

Industry, too, promoted health and well being. The active man goes to bed tired every night; his rest is sound and sweet, and he wakes up early in the morning, fresh and strong for another day's delightful toil. His appetite and digestion are good. He has an excellent sauce in recreation, and a good tonic in toil. What companionship can such a man have with moping and melancholy? Such morbid spirits hang around those who do little and dine excessively. People who make themselves useful to the community, receive back from the community their full share of health, happiness, and prosperity. They brighten the daily task, and keep the world moving. They are the gold of the nation and the salt of the earth.

"Earnestness," said a Great Teacher, "is the path of immortality. They who are in earnest do not die; they who are not in earnest are as if dead already." Earnestness is the dedication of the entire mind to its task. We live only in what we do. Earnest people are dissatisfied with anything short of the highest excellence in whatever they do, and they always reach that excellence. They are so many that are careless and half hearted, so satisfied with a poor performance, that the earnest ones shine apart as it were, in their excellence. They are always plenty of "vacancies" in the ranks of usefulness and service for earnest people. There never was, and never will be, a deeply earnest man or woman who did not fill successfully some suitable sphere. Such people are scrupulous, conscientious, and painstaking, and cannot rest in ease until the very best is done, and the whole world is always on the lookout to reward the best. It always stands ready to pay the full price, whether in money, fame, friends, influence, happiness, scope or life, for that which is of surpassing excellence, whether it be in things material, intellectual, or spiritual. What ever you are – whether shopkeeper or saintly teacher you can safely give the very best to the world without any doubt or misgiving. If the indelible impress of your earnestness be on your goods in the one case, or on your words in the other, your business will flourish, or your precepts will live.

Earnest people make rapid progress both in their work and their character. It is thus that they live, and "do not die," for stagnation only is death, and where there is incessant progress and ever ascending excellence, stagnation and health are swallowed up in activity and life.

Thus is the making and masonry of the First pillar explained. He who builds it well, and sets it firm and straight, will have a powerful and enduring support in the business of his life.

Second Pillar – Economy

It is said of Nature that she knows on vacuum. She also knows no waste. In the divine economy my Nature everything is conserved and turned to good account. Even excreta are chemically transmitted, and utilized in the building up of new forms. Nature destroys every foulness, not by annihilation, but by transmutation, by sweetening and purifying it, and making it serve the ends of things beautiful, useful and good.

That economy which, in nature is a universal principle, is in man a moral quality and it is that quality by which he preserves his energies, and sustains his place as a working unit in the scheme of things.

Financial economy is merely a fragment of this principle, or rather it is a material symbol of that economy which is purely mental, and its transmutations spiritual. The financial economist exchanges coppers for silver, silver for gold, gold for notes, and the notes he converts into the figures of a bank account. By these conversions of money into more readily transmissible forms he is the gainer in the financial management of his affairs. The spiritual economist transmutes passions into intelligence, intelligence into principles, principles into wisdom, and wisdom is manifested in actions which are few but of powerful effect. By all these transmutations he is the gainer in character and in the management of his life.

True economy is the middle way in all things, whether material or mental, between waste and undue retention. That which is wasted, whether money or mental energy, is rendered powerless; that which is selfishly retained and hoarded up, is equally powerless. To secure power, whether of capital or mentality, there must be concentration, but concentration must be followed by legitimate use. The gathering up of money or energy is only a means; the end is use; and it is use only that produces power.

An all round economy consists in finding the middle way in the following seven things:— Money, Food, Clothing, Recreation, Rest, Time and Energy.

Money is the symbol of exchange, and represents purchasing power. He who is anxious to acquire financial wealth as well as he who wishes to avoid debt – must study how to apportion, his expenditure in accordance with his income, so as to leave a margin of ever increasing working capital, or to have a little store ready in hand for any emergency. Money spent in thoughtless expenditure – in worthless pleasures or harmful luxuries – is money wasted and power destroyed; for, although a limited and subordinate power, the means and capacity for legitimate and virtuous purchase is, nevertheless, a power, and one that enters largely into the details of our everyday life. The spendthrift can never become rich, but if he begin with riches, must soon become poor. The miser, with all his stored-away gold, cannot be said to be rich, for he is in want, and his gold, lying idle, is deprived of its power of purchase. The thrifty and prudent are on the way to riches, for while they spend wisely they save carefully, and gradually enlarge their spheres as their growing means allow.

The poor man who is to become rich must begin at the bottom, and must not wish, nor try to appear affluent by attempting something far beyond his means. There is always plenty of room and scope at the bottom, and it is a safe place from which to begin, as there is nothing below, and everything above. Many a young business man comes at once to grief by swagger and display which he foolishly imagines are necessary to success, but which, deceiving no one but himself, lead quickly to ruin. A modest and true beginning, in any sphere, will better ensure success than an exaggerated advertisement of one's standing and importance. The smaller the capital, the smaller should be the sphere of operations. Capital and scope are hand and glove, and they should fit. Concentrate your capital within the circle of its working power, and however circumscribed that circle may be it will continue to widen and extend as the gathering momentum of power presses for expression.

Above all take care always to avoid the two extremes of parsimony and prodigality.

Food represents life, vitality, and both physical and mental strength. There is a middle way in eating and drinking, as in all else. The man who is to achieve prosperity must be well nourished, but not overfed. The man that starves his body, whether through miserliness or asceticism (both forms of false economy), diminishes his mental energy, and renders his body too enfeebled to be the instrument for any strong achievement. Such a man courts sickly mindedness, a condition conducive only to failure.

The glutton, however, destroys himself by excess. His bestialized body becomes a stored up reservoir of poisons, which attract disease and corruption, while his mind becomes more and more brutalized and confused, and therefore more incapable. Gluttony is one of the lowest and most animal vices, and is obnoxious to all who pursue a moderate course.

The best workers and most successful men are they who are most moderate in eating and drinking. By taking enough nourishment, but not too much, they attain the maximum physical and mental fitness. Beings thus well equipped by moderation, they are enabled to vigorously and joyfully fight the battle of life.

Clothing is covering and protection for the body, though it is frequently wrested from this economic purpose, and made a means of vain display. The two extremes to be avoided here are negligence and vanity. Custom cannot, and need not, be ignored; and cleanliness is all important. The ill-dressed, unkempt man or woman invites failure and loneliness. A man's dress should harmonize with his station in life, and it should be of good quality, and be well made and appropriate. Clothing should not be cast aside while comparatively new, but should be well worn. If a man be poor, he will not lose in either self respect or the respect of others by wearing threadbare clothing if it be clean and his whole body be clean and neat. But vanity, leading to excessive luxury in clothing, is a vice which should be studiously avoided by virtuous people. I know a lady who had forty dresses in her wardrobe; also a man who had twenty walking-sticks, about the same number of hats, and some dozen mackintoshes; while another had some twenty or thirty pairs of boots. Rich people who thus squander money on piles of superfluous clothing, are courting poverty, for it is waste, and waste leads to want. The money so heedlessly spent could be better used, for suffering abounds and charity is noble.

An obtrusive display in clothing and jewellery bespeaks a vulgar and empty mind. Modest and cultured people are modest and becoming in their dress, and their spare money is wisely used in further enhancing their culture and virtue. Education and progress are of more importance to them than vain and needless apparel; and literature, art, and science are encouraged thereby. A true refinement is in the mind and behaviour, and a mind adorend with virtue and intelligence cannot add to its attractiveness though it may detract from it) by an ostentatious display of the body. Time spent in uselessly adorning the body could be more fruitfully employed. Simplicity in dress, as in other things, is the best. It touches the point of excellence in usefulness, comfort, and bodily grace, and bespeaks true taste and cultivated refinement.

Recreation is one of the necessities of life. Every man and women should have some definitive work as the main object of life, and to which a considerable amount of time should be devoted, and he should only turn from it at given and limited periods for recreation and rest. The object of recreation is greater buoyancy of both body and mind, with an increase of power in one's serious work. It is, therefore, a means, not an end; and this should ever be born in mind, for, to many, some forms of recreation innocent and good in themselves – become so fascinating that they are in danger of making them the end of life, and of thus abandoning duty for pleasure. To make of life a ceaseless round of games and pleasures, with no other object in life, is to turn living upside down, as it were, and it produces monotony and enervation. People who do it are the most unhappy of mortals, and suffer from languor, ennui, and peevishness. As sauce is an aid to digestion, and can only lead to misery when made the work of life. When a man has done his day's duty he can turn to his recreation with a free mind and a light heart, and both his work and his pleasure will be to him a source of happiness.

It is a true economy in this particular neither to devote the whole of one's time to work nor to recreation, but to apportion to each its time and place; and so fill out life with those changes which are necessary to a long life and a fruitful existence.

All agreeable changes is recreation and the mental worker will gain both in the quality and, quantity of his work by laying it down at the time appointed for restful and refreshing recreation; while the physical worker will improve in every way by turning to some form of study as a hobby or means of education.

As we do not spend all our time in eating or sleeping or resting, neither should we spend it in exercise or pleasure, but should give recreation its proper place as a natural tonic in the economic scheme of our life.

Rest is for recuperation after toil. Every self respecting human being should do sufficient work every day to make his sleep restful and sweet, and his rising up fresh and bright.

Enough sleep should be taken, but not too much, over indulgence on the one hand, or deprivation on the other, are both harmful. It is an easy matter to find out how much sleep one requires. By going to bed early, and getting up early (rising a little earlier every morning if one has been in the habit of spending long hours in bed), one can very soon accurately gauge and adjust the number of hours he or she requires for complete recuperation. It will be found as the sleeping hours are shortened that the sleep becomes more and more sound and sweet, and the waking up more and more alert and bright. People who are to prosper in their work must not give way to ignoble ease and over indulgence in sleep. Fruitful labour, and not ease, is the true end of life, and ease is only good in so far as it sub-serves the ends of work. Sloth and prosperity can never be companions can never even approach each other. The sluggard will never overtake success, but failure will speedily catch up with him, and leave him defeated. Rest is to fit us for greater labour, and not to pamper us in indolence. When the bodily vigour is restored, the end of rest is accomplished. A perfect balance between labour and rest contributes considerably to health, happiness, and prosperity.

Time is that which we all possess in equal measure. The day is not lengthened for any man. We should therefore see to it that we do not squander its precious minutes in unprofitable waste. He who spends his time in self indulgence and the pursuit of pleasure, presently finds himself old, and nothing has been accomplished. He who fills full with useful pursuits the minutes as they come and go, grows old in honour and wisdom, and prosperity abides with him. Money wasted can be restored; health wasted can be restored; but time wasted can never be restored.

It is an old saying that "time is money." It is, in the same way, health, and strength, and talent, and genius, and wisdom, in accordance with the manner in which it is used; and to properly use it, the minutes must be seized upon as they come, for once they are past they can never be recalled. The day should be divided into portions, and everything – work, leisure, meals, recreation – should be attend to in its proper time; and the time of preparation should not be overlooked or ignored. Whatever a man does, he will do it better and more successfully by utilizing some small portion of the day in preparing his mind for his work. The man who gets up early in order to think and plan, that he may weigh and consider and forecast, will always manifest greater skill and success in his particular pursuit, than the man who lives in bed till the last moment, and only gets up just in time to begin breakfast. An hour spend in this way before breakfast will prove of the greatest value in making one's efforts fruitful. It is a means of calming and clarifying the mind, and of focussing one's energies so as to render them more powerful and effective. The best and most abiding success is that which is made before eight o'clock in the morning. He who is at his business at six o'clock, will always other conditions being equal be a long way ahead of the man who is in bed at eight. The lie a bed heavily handicaps himself in the race of life. He gives his early-rising competitor two or three hours start every day. How can he ever hope to win with such a self imposed tax upon his time? At the end of a year that two or three hours start every day is shown in a success which is the synthesis of accumulated results. What, then, must be the difference between the efforts of these two men at the end, say, of twenty years! The lie-a-bed, too, after he gets up is always in a hurry trying to regain lost time, which results in more loss of time, for hurry always defeats its own end. The early rise, who thus economies his time, has no need to hurry, for he is always ahead of the hour, is always well up with his work; he can well afford to be calm and deliberate, and to do carefully and well whatever is in hand, for his good habit shows itself at the end of the day in the form of a happy frame of mind, and in bigger results in the shape of work skillfully and successfully done.

In the economizing of time, too, there will be many things which a man will have to eliminate from his life; some of things and pursuits which he loves, and desires to retain, will have to be sacrifice to the main purpose of his life. The studied elimination of non-essentials from one's daily life is a vital factor in all great achievement. All great men are adepts in this branch of economy, and it plays an important part in the making of their greatness. It is a form of economy which also enters into the mind, the actions, and the speech, eliminating from them all that is superfluous, and that impedes, and does not sub-serve, the end aimed at. Foolish and unsuccessful people talk carelessly and aimlessly, act carelessly and aimlessly, and allow everything that comes along good, bad, and different to lodge in their mind.

The mind of the true economist is a sieve which lets everything fall through except that which is of use to him in the business of his life. He also employs only necessary words, and does only necessary actions, thus vastly minimizing friction and waste of power.

To go to bed betime and to get up betime, to fill in every working minute with purposeful thought and effective action, this is the true economy of time.

Energy is economized by the formation of good habits. All vices are a reckless expenditure of energy. Sufficient energy is thoughtlessly wasted in bad habits to enable men to accomplish the greatest success, if conserved and used in right directions. If economy be practiced in the six points already considered, much will be done in the conservation of one's energies, but a man must go still further, and carefully husband his vitality by the avoidance of all forms of physical self indulgences and impurities, but also all those mental vices such as hurry, worry, excitement, despondency, anger, complaining and envy – which deplete the mind and render it unfit for any important work or admirable achievement. They are common forms of mental dissipation which a man of character should study how to avoid and overcome. The energy wasted in frequent fits of bad temper would, if controlled and properly directed, give a man strength of mind, force of character, and much power to achieve. The angry man is a strong man made weak by the dissipation of his mental energy. He needs self control to manifest his strength. The calm man is always his superior in any department of life, and will always take precedence of him, both in his success, and in the estimation of others. No man can afford to disperse his energies in fostering bad habits and bad tendencies of mind. Every vice, however, apparently small will tell against him in the battle of life. Every harmful self indulgence will come back to him in the form of some trouble or weakness. Every moment of riot or of pandering to his lower inclinations will make his progress more laborious, and will hold him back from scaling the high heaven of his wishes for achievement. On the other hand, he who economizes his energies, and bends them towards the main task of his life, will make rapid progress, and nothing will prevent him from reaching the golden city of success.

It will be seen that economy is something far more profound and far reaching than the mere saving of money. It touches every part of our nature and every phase of our life. The old saying, "Take care of the pence, and the pounds will take care of themselves," may be regarded as a parable, for the lower passions as native energy; it is the abuse of that energy that is bad, and if this personal energy be taken care of and stored up and transmuted, it reappears as force of character. To waste this valuable energy in the pursuit of vice is like wasting the pence, and so losing the pounds, but to take care of it for good uses is to store up the pence of passions, and so gain the golden pounds of good. Take care, therefore, of the lower energies, and the higher achievements will take care of themselves.

The Pillar of Economy, when soundly built, will be found to be composed largely of these four qualities:—

1. Moderation
2. Efficiency
3. Resourcefulness
4. Originality

Moderation is the strong core of economy. It avoids extremes, finding the middle way in all things. It also consists in abstaining from the unnecessary and the harmful. There can be no such things as moderation in that which is evil, for that would be excess. A true moderation abstains from evil. It is not a moderate use of fire to put our hands into it, but to warm them by it at a safe distance. Evil is a fire that will burn a man though he but touch it. a harmful luxury is best left severely alone. Smoking, snuff taking, alcoholic drinking, gambling, and other such common vices, although they have dragged thousands down to ill health, misery, and failure, have never helped one towards health, happiness and success. The man who eschews them will always be head of the man that pursues them, their talents and opportunities being equal. Healthy, happy, and long lived people are always moderate and abstemious in their habits. By moderation the life forces are preserved; by excess they are destroyed. Men, also, who carry moderation into their thoughts, allaying their passions and feelings, avoiding all unwholesome extremes and morbid sensations and sentiments, add knowledge and wisdom to happiness and health, and thereby attain to the highest felicity and power. The immoderate destroy themselves by their own folly. They weaken their energies and stultify their capabilities, and instead of achieving an abiding success, reach only, at best, a fitful and precarious prosperity.

Efficiency proceeds from the right conservation of one's forces and powers. All skill is the use of concentrated energy. Superior skill, as talent and genius, is a higher degree of concentrated force. Men are always skillful in that which they love, because the mind is almost ceaselessly centered upon it. Skill is the result of that mental economy which transmutes thought into invention and action. There will be no prosperity without skill, and one's prosperity will be in the measure of one's skill. By a process of natural selection, the inefficient fall in to their right places. Among the badly paid or unemployed; for who will employ a man who cannot, or will not, do his work properly? An employer may occasionally keep such a man out of charity; but this will be exceptional; as places of business, offices, households, and all centers of organized activity, are not charitable institutions, but industrial bodies which stand or fall but the fitness and efficiency of their individual members.

Skill is gained by thoughtfulness and attention. Aimless and inattentive people are usually out of employment – to wit, the lounger at the street corner. They cannot do the simplest thing properly, because they will not rouse up the mind to thought and attention. Recently an acquaintance of mine employed a tramp to clean his windows, but the man had refrained from work and systematic thought for so long that he had become incapable of both, and could not even clean a window. Even when shown how to do it, he could not follow the simple instructions given. This is an instance, too, of the fact that the simplest thing requires a measure of skill in the doing. Efficiency largely determines a man's place among his fellows, and leads one on by steps to higher and higher positions as greater powers are developed. The good workman is skillful, with his tools, while the good man is skillful with his thoughts. Wisdom is the highest form of skill. Aptitude in incipient wisdom. There is one right way of doing everything, even the smallest, and a thousand wrong ways. Skill consists in finding the one right way, and adhering to it. The inefficient bungle confusedly about among the thousand wrong ways, and do not adopt the right even when it is pointed out to them. They do this in some cases because they think, in their ignorance, that they know best, thereby placing themselves in a position where it becomes impossible to learn, even though it be only to learn how to clean a window or sweep a floor. Thoughtlessness and inefficiency are all too common. There is plenty of room in the world for common. There is plenty of room in the world for thoughtful and efficient people. Employers of labour know how difficult it is to get the best workmanship. The good workman, whether with tools or brain, whether with speech or thought, will always find a place for the exercise of his skill.

Resourcefulness is the outcome of efficiency. It is an important element in prosperity, for the resourceful man is never confounded. He may have many falls, but he will always be equal to the occasion, and will be on his feet again immediately. Resourcefulness has its fundamental cause in the conservation of energy. It is energy transmuted. When a man cuts off certain mental or bodily vices which have been depleting him of his energy, what becomes of the energy so conserved? It is not destroyed or lost, for energy can never be destroyed or lost. It becomes productive energy. It reappears in the form of fruitful thought. The virtuous man is always more successful than the vicious man because he is teeming with resources. His entire mentality is alive and vigorous, abounding with stored up energy. What the vicious man wastes in barren indulgence, the virtuous man uses in fruitful industry. A new life and a new world, abounding with all fascinating pursuits and pure delights, open up to the man who shuts himself off from the old world of animal vice, and his place will be assured by the resources which will well up within him. Barren seed perishes in the earth; there is no place for it in the fruitful economy of nature. Barren minds sink in the struggle of life. Human society makes for good, and there is no room in it for the emptiness engendered by vice. But the barren mind will not sink for ever. When it wills, it can become fruitful and regain itself. By the very nature of existence, by the eternal law of progress, the vicious man must fall; but having fallen, he can rise again. He can turn from vice to virtue, and stand, self respecting and secure, upon his own resources.

The resourceful men invent, discover, initiate. They cannot fail, for they are in the stream of progress. They are full of new schemes, new methods, new hopes, and their life is so much fuller and richer thereby. They are men of supple minds. When a man fails to improve his business, his work, his methods, he falls out of the line of progress, and has begun to fail. His mind has become stiff and inert like the body of an aged man, and so fails to keep pace with the rapidly moving ideas and plans of resourceful minds. A resourceful mind is like a river which never runs dry, and which affords refreshment, and supplies new vigour, in times of drought. Men of resources are men of new ideas, and men of new ideas flourish where others fade and decay.

Originality is resourcefulness ripened and perfected. Where there is originality there is genius, and men of genius are the lights of the world. Whatever work a man does, he should fall back upon his own resources in the doing it. While learning from others, he should not slavishly imitate them, but should put himself into his work, and so make it new and original. Original men get the ear of the world. They may be neglected at first, but they are always ultimately accepted, and become patterns for mankind. Once a man has acquired the knack of originality, he takes his place as a leader among men in his particular department of knowledge and skill. But originality cannot be forced; it can only be developed; and it is developed by proceeding from excellence to excellence, by ascending in the scale of skill by the full and right use of one's mental powers. Let a man consecrate himself to his work, let him, so consecrated, concentrate all his energies upon it, and the day will come when the world will hail him as one of its strong sons; and he, too, like Balzac who, after many years of strenuous toil, one day exclaimed, "I am about to become a genius!, "I am about to become a genius" will at least discover, to his joy, that he has joined the company of original minds, the gods who lead mankind into newer, higher, and more beneficent ways.

The composition of the Second Pillar is thus revealed. Its building awaits the ready work man who will skillfully apply his mental energies.

Third Pillar – Integrity

There is no striking a cheap bargain with prosperity. It must be purchased, not only with intelligent labor, but with moral force. as the bubble cannot endure, so the fraud cannot prosper. He makes a feverish spurt in the acquirement of money, and then collapses. Nothing is ever gained, ever can be gained, by fraud. It is but wrested for a time, to be again returned with heavy interest. But fraud is not confined to the unscrupulous swindler. All who are getting, or trying to get, money without giving an equivalent are practicing fraud, whether they know it or not. Men who are anxiously scheming how to get money without working for it, are frauds, and mentally they are closely allied to the thief and swindler under whose influence they come, sooner or later, and who deprives them of their capital. What is a thief but a man who carries to its logical or later, and who deprives them of their capital. What is a thief but a man who carries to its logical extreme the desire to possess without giving a just return – that is, unlawfully? The man that courts prosperity must, in all his transactions, whether material or mental, study how to give a just return for that which he receives. This is the great fundamental principle in all sound commerce, while in spiritual things it becomes the doing to others that which we would have them do to us, and applied to the forces of the universe, it is scientifically stated in the formula, "Action and Reaction are equal."

Human life is reciprocal, not rapacious, and the man who regards all others as his legitimate prey will soon find himself stranded in the desert of ruin, far away from the path of prosperity. He is too far behind in the process of evolution to cope successfully with honest man. The fittest, the best, always survive, and he being the worst, cannot therefore continue. His end, unless the change in time, is sure it is the goal, the filthy hovel, or the place of the deserted outcast. His efforts are destructive, and not constructive, and he thereby destroys himself.

It was Carlyle who, referring to Mohammed being then universally regarded by Christians as an impostor, exclaimed, "An impostor found a religion! An impostor couldn't built a brick house" an impostor, a liar a cheat the man of dishonesty cannot build as he has neither tools or material with which to build. He can no more build up a business, a character, a career, a success, than he can found a religion or build a brick house. He not only does not build, but all his energies are bent on undermining what others have built, but his being impossible, he undermines himself.

Without integrity, energy and economy will at last fail, but aided by integrity, their strength will be greatly augmented. There is not an occasion in life in which the moral factor does not play an important part. Sterling integrity tell wherever it is, and stamps it hall mark on all transactions; and it does this because of its wonderful coherence and consistency, and its invincible strength. For the man of integrity is in line with the fixed laws of things – not only with the fundamental principles on which human society rests, but with the laws which hold the vast universe together. Who shall set these at naught? Who, then, shall undermine the man of unblemished integrity? He is like a strong tree whose roots are fed by perennial springs, and which no tempest can law low.

To be complete and strong, integrity must embrace the whole man, and extend to all the details of his life; and it must be so through and permanent as to withstand all temptations to swerve into compromise. To fail in one point is to fail in all, and to admit, under stress, a compromise with falsehood, howsoever necessary and insignificant it may appear, is to throw down the shield of integrity, and to stand exposed to the onslaughts of evil.

The man who works as carefully and conscientiously when his employer is away as when his eye is upon him, will not long remain in an inferior position. Such integrity in duty, in performing the details of his work, will quickly lead him into the fertile regions of prosperity.

The shirker, on the other hand – he who does not scruple to neglect his work when his employer is not about, thereby robbing his employer of the time and labour for which he is paid – will quickly come to the barren region of unemployment, and will look in vain for needful labour.

There will come a time, too, to the man who is not deeply rooted in integrity, when it will seem necessary to his prospects and prosperity that he should tell a lie or do a dishonest thing – I say, to the man who is not deeply rooted in this principle, for a man of fixed and enlightened integrity knows that lying and dishonesty can never under any circumstance be necessary, and therefore he neither needs to be tempted in this particular, nor can he possibly be tempted but the one so tempted must be able to cast aside the subtle insinuation of falsehood which, in a time of indecision and perplexity, arises within him, and he must stand firmly by the principle, being willing to lose and suffer rather than sink into obliquity. In this way only can he become enlightened concerning this moral principle, and discover the glad truth that integrity does not lead to loss and suffering, but to gain and joy; that honesty and deprivation are not, and cannot be, related as cause and effect.

It is this willingness to sacrifice rather than be untrue that leads to enlightenment in all spheres of life; and the man who, rather than sacrifice some selfish aim, will lie or deceive, has forfeited his right to moral enlighten-ment, and takes his place lower down among the devotees of deceit, among the doers of shady transactions, than men of no character and no reputation.

A man is not truly armoured with integrity until he has become incapable of lying or deceiving either by gesture, word, or act; until he sees, clearly, openly, and freed from all doubt, the deadly effects of such moral turpitude. The man so enlightened is protect from all quarters, and can no more be undermined by dishonest men than the sun can be pulled down from heaven by madmen, and the arrows of selfishness and treachery that may be poured upon him will rebound from the strong armour of his integrity and the bright shield of his righteousness, leaving him unharmed and untouched.

A lying tradesman will tell you that no man can thrive and be honest in these days of keen competition. How can such a man know this, seeing that he has never tried honest? Moreover, such a man has no knowledge of honesty, and his statement is therefore, a statement of ignorance, and ignorance and falsehood so blind a man that he foolishly imagines all are as ignorant and false as himself. I have known such tradesmen, and have seen them come to ruin. I once heard a businessman make the following statement in a public meeting:—"No man can be entirely honest in business; he can only be approximately honest." He imagined that his statement revealed the condition of the business world; it did not, it revealed his own condition. He was merely telling his audience that he was a dishonest man, but his ignorance, moral ignorance, prevented him from seeing this. Approximate honesty is only another term for dishonesty. The man who deviated a little from the straight path, will deviate more. He has no fixed principle of right and is only thinking of his own advantage. That he persuades himself that his particular dishonesty is of a white and harmless kind, and that he is not so bad as his neighbour, is only of the many forms of self delusion which ignorance of moral principles creates.

Right doing between man and main in the varied relations and transactions of life is the very soul of integrity. It includes, but is more than, honesty. It is the backbone of human society, and the support of human institutions.

Without it there would be no trust, no confidence between men, and the business world would topple to its fall.

As the liar thinks all men are liars, and treats them as such, so the man of integrity treats all men with confidence. He trusts them, and they trust him. His clear eye and open hand shame the creeping fraud so that he cannot practice his fraud on him. As Emerson has so finely put it – "Trust men and they will be true to you, even though they make an exception in your favor to al their rules of trade."

The upright man by his very presence commands the morality of those about him making them better than they were. Men are powerfully influenced by one another, and, as good is more powerful than evil, the strong and good man both shames and elevates, by his contact, the weak and bad.

The man of integrity carries about with him an unconscious grandeur which both awes and inspires. Having lifted himself above the petty, the mean, and the false, those coward vices slink from his presence in confusion. The highest intellectual gift cannot compare with this lofty moral grandeur. In the memory of men and the estimation of the world the man of integrity occupies a higher place than the man of genius. Buckminster says, "The moral grandeur of an independent integrity is the sublimest thing in nature." It is the quality in man which produces heroes. The man of unswerving rectitude is, intrinsically, always a hero. It only needs the occasion to bring out the heroic element. He is always, too, possessed a permanent happiness. The man of genius may be very unhappy, but not to the man of integrity. Nothing nor sickness, nor calamity, nor death – can deprive him of that permanent satisfaction which inheres in uprightness.

Rectitude leads straight to prosperity by four successive steps. First, the upright man wins the confidence of others. Second, having gained their confidence, they put trust in him. Third, this trust, never being violated, produces a good reputation; and fourth, a good reputation spreads further and further, and so bring about success.

Dishonesty has the reverse effect. By destroying the confidence of others, it produces in them suspicion and mistrust, and these bring about a bad reputation, which culminates in failure.

The Pillar of Integrity is held together by these four virile elements:

1. Honesty
2. Fearlessness
3. Purposefulness
4. Invincibility

Honesty is the surest way to success. The day at last comes when the dishonest man repents in sorrow and suffering: but not man ever needs to repent of having been honest. Even when the honest man fails – as he does sometimes, through lacking other of these pillars, such as energy, economy, or system his failure is not the grievous thing it is to the dishonest man, for he can always rejoice in the fact that he has never defrauded a fellow being. Even in his darkest hour he finds repose in a clear conscience.

Ignorant men imagine that dishonesty is a short cut to prosperity. This is why they practice it. The dishonest man is morally short sighted. Like the drunkard who sees the immediate pleasure of his habit, but not the ultimate degradation, he sees the immediate effect of a dishonest act – a larger profit but not its ultimate outcome; he does not see that an accumulated number of such acts must inevitably undermine his character, and bring his business toppling about his ears in ruin. While pocketing his gains, and thinking how cleverly and successfully he is imposing on others, he is all the time imposing on himself, and every coin thus gained must be paid back with added interest, and from this just retribution there is no possible loophole of escape. This moral gravitation is an sure and unvarying as the physical gravitation of a stone to the earth.

The tradesman who demands of his assistants that they shall be, and misrepresents his goods to customers, is surrounding himself on all hands with suspicion, mistrust, and hatred. Even the moral weaklings who carry out his instructions, despise him while defiling themselves with his unclean work. How can success thrive in such a poisonous atmosphere? The spirit of ruin is already in such a business, and the day of his fall is ordained.

An honest man may fail, but not because he is honest, and his failure will be honourable, and will not injure his character and reputation. His failure, too, resulting doubtless from his incapacity in the particular direction of his failure, will be a means of leading him into something more suited to his talents, and thus to ultimate success.

Fearlessness accompanies honesty. The honest man has a clear eye and an unflinching gaze. He looks his fellowmen in the face, and his speech is direct and convincing. The liar and cheat hangs his head; his eye is muddy and his gaze oblique. He cannot look another man in the eye, and his speech arouses mistrust, for it is ambiguous and unconvincing.

When a man has fulfilled his obligations, he has nothing to fear. All his business relations are safe and secure. His methods and actions will endure the light of day. Should he pass through a difficult time, and, get into debt, everybody will trust him and be willing to wait for payment, and all his debts will be paid. Dishonest people try to avoid paying their debts, and they live in fear; but the honest man tries to avoid getting into debt, but when debt overtakes him, he does not fear, but, redoubling his exertions, his debts are paid.

The dishonest are always in fear. They do not fear debt, but fear that they will have to pay their debts. They fear their fellow-men, fear the established authorities, fear the results of all that they do, and they are in constant fear of their misdeeds being revealed, and of the consequences which may at any moment overtake them.

The honest man is rid of all this burden of fear. He is light hearted, and walks erect among his fellows; not assuming a part, and skulking and cringing, but being himself, and meeting eye to eye. Not deceiving or injuring any, there are none to fear, and anything and against him can only rebound to his advantage.

And this fearlessness is, in itself, a tower to strength in a man's life, supporting him through all emergencies, enabling him to battle manfully with difficulties, and in the end securing for him that success of which he cannot be dispossessed.

Purposefulness is the direct outcome of that strength of character which integrity fosters. The man of integrity is the man of direct aims and strong and intelligent purposes. He does not guess, and work in the dark. All his plans have in them some of that moral fiber of which his character is wrought. A man's work will always in some way reflect himself, and the man of sound integrity is the man of sound plan. He weights and considers and looks ahead, and so is less likely to make serious mistakes, or to bungle into a dilemma from which it is difficult to escape. Taking a moral view of all things, and always considering moral consequences, he stands on a firmer and more exalted ground than the man of mere policy and expedience; and while commanding a more extended view of any situation, he wields the greater power which a more comprehensive grasp of details with the principles involved, confers upon him. Morality always has the advantage of expediency. Its purposes always reach down far below the surface, and are therefore more firm and secure, more strong and lasting. There is a native directness, too, about integrity, which enables the man to get straight to the mark in whatever he does, and which makes failure almost impossible.

Strong men have strong purposes, and strong purposes lead to strong achievements. The man of integrity is above all men strong, and his strength is manifested in that thoroughness with which he does the business of his life; thoroughness which commands respect, admiration, and success.

Invincibility is a glorious protector, but it only envelopes the man whose integrity is perfectly pure and unassailable. Never to violate, even in the most insignificant particular, the principle of integrity, is to be invincible against all the assaults of innuendo, slander, and misrepresentation. The man who has failed in one point is vulnerable, and the shaft of evil, entering that point, will lay him low, like the arrow in the heel of Achilles. Pure and perfect integrity is proof against all attack and injury, enabling its possessor to meet all opposition and persecution with dauntless courage and sublime equanimity. No amount of talent, intellect, or business acumen can give a man that power of mind and peace of heart which come from an enlightened acceptance and observance of lofty moral principles. Moral force is the greatest power. Let the seeker for a true prosperity discover this force, let him foster and develop it in his mind and in his deeds, and as he succeeds he will take his place among the strong leaders of the earth.

Such is the strong and adamantine Pillar of integrity. Blessed and prosperous above all men will be he who builds its incorruptible masonry into the temple of his life.

Fourth Pillar – System

System is that principle of order by which confusion is rendered impossible. In the natural and universal order everything is in its place, so that the vast universe runs more perfectly than the most perfect machine. Disorder in space would mean the destruction of the universe; and disorder in a man's affairs destroys his work and his prosperity.

All complex organizations are built up by system. No business or society can develop into large dimensions apart from system, and this principle is preeminently the instrument of the merchant, the business man, and the organizer of institutions.

There are many departments in which a disorderly man may succeed – although attention to order would increase his success but he will not succeed in business unless he can place the business entirely in the hands of a systematic manager, who will thereby remedy his own defect.

All large business concerns have been evolved along definitely drawn systematic lines, any violation of which would be disastrous to the efficiency and welfare of the business. Complex business or other organizations are built up like complex bodies in nature, by scrupulous attention to details. The disorderly man thinks he can be careless about every thing but the main end, but by ignoring the means he frustrates the end. By the disarrangement of details, organisms perish, and by the careless neglect of details, the growth of any work or concern is prevented.

Disorderly people waste an enormous amount of time and energy. The time frittered away in hunting for things is sufficient, were if conserved by order, to enable them to achieve any success, for slovenly people never have a place for anything, and have to hunt, frequently for a long time, for any article which they require. In the irritation, bad humour, and chagrin which this daily hunting for things brings about, as much energy is dissipated as would be required to build up a big business, or scale the highest heights of achievement in any direction.

Orderly people conserve both their time and energy. They never lose anything, and therefore never have to find anything. Everything is in its place, and the hand can be at once placed upon it, though it be in the dark. They can well afford to be cool and deliberate and so use their mental energies in something more profitable than irritation, bad temper and accusing others for their own lack of order.

There is a kind of genius in system which can perform apparent wonders with ease. A systematic man can get through so great a quantity of work in such a short time, and with such freedom from such exhaustion, as to appear almost miraculous. He scale the heights of success while his slovenly competitor is wallowing hopelessly in the bogs of confusion. His strict observance of the law of order enables him to reach his ends, swiftly and smoothly, without friction or loss of time.

The demands of system, in all departments of the business world, are as rigid and exacting as the holy vows of a saint, and cannot be violated in the smallest particular but at the risk of one's financial prospects. In the financial world, the law of order is an iron necessity, and he who faultlessly observes it, saves time, temper, and money.

Every enduring achievement in human society rests upon a basis of system; so true is this, that were system withdrawn, progress would cease. Think, for instance, of the vast achievements of literature the works of classic authors and of great geniuses; the great poems, the innumerable prose works, the monumental histories, the soul – stirring orations; think also the social intercourse of human society, of it religions, its legal statutes, and its vast fund of book knowledge think of all these wonderful resources and achievements of language, and then reflect that they all depend for their origin, growth, and continuance on the systematic arrangements of twenty six letters, an arrangement having inexhaustible and illimitable results by the fact of its rigid limitation within certain fixed rules.

Again; all the wonderful achievements of mathematics have come from the systematic arrangement of ten figures; while the most complex piece of machinery, with its thousands of parts working together smoothly and almost noiselessly to the achievement of the end for which it was designed, was brought forth by the systematic observance of a few mechanical laws.

Herein we see how system simplifies that is complex: how it makes easy that which was difficult; how it relates an infinite variety of details of the one central law or order, and so enables them to be dealt with and accounted for with perfect regularity, and with an entire absence of confusion.

The scientist names and classifies the myriad details of the universe, from the microscopic rotifer to the telescopic star, by his observance of the principle of system, so that out of many millions of objects, reference can be made to any one object in, at most, a few minutes. It is this faculty of speedy references and swift dispatch which is of such overwhelming importance in every department of knowledge and industry, and the amount of time and labour thus saved to humanity is so vast as to be incompatible. We speak of religious, political, and business systems; and so on, indicating that all things in human society are welded together by the adhesive qualities of order.

System is, indeed, one of the great fundamental principles in progress, and in the binding together, in one complete whole, of the world's millions of human beings while they are at the same time each striving for a place and are competing with one another in opposing aims and interest.

We see here how system is allied with greatness, for the many separate units whose minds are untrained to the discipline of system, are kept in their places by the organizing power of the comparatively few who perceive the urgent, the inescapable, necessity for the establishment of fixed and inviolable rules, whether in business, law, religion, science, or politics in fact, in every sphere of human activity for immediately two human beings meet together, they need some common ground of understanding for the avoidance of confusion; in a word, some system to regulate their actions.

Life is too short for confusion; and knowledge grows and progress proceeds along avenues of system which prevent retardation and retrogression, so that he who systematizes his knowledge or business, simplifies and enhances it for his successor, enabling him to begin, with a free mind, where he left off.

Every large business has its system which renders its vast machinery workable, enabling it to run like a well balanced and well oiled machine. A remarkable business man, a friend of mine, once told me that he could have his huge business for twelve months, and it would run on without hitch till his return; and he does occasionally leave it for several months, while travelling, and on his return, every man, boy and girl; every tool, book, and machine; every detail down to the smallest, is in its place doing its work as when he left; and no trouble, no difficulty, no confusion has arisen.

There can be no marked success part from a love of regularity and discipline, and the avoidance of friction, along with the restfulness and efficiency of mind which spring from such regularity. People who abhor discipline, whose minds are ungoverned and anarchic, and who are careless and irregular in their thinking, their habits and the management of their affairs, cannot be highly successful and prosperous, and they fill their lives with numerous worries, troubles, difficulties, and petty annoyances, all of which would disappear under a proper regulation of their lives.

An unsystematic mind is an untrained mind and it can no more cope with well disciplined minds in the race of life than an untrained athlete can successfully complete with a carefully trained competitor in athletic competitor in athletic races. The ill disciplined mind, that thinks anything will do, rapidly falls behind the well disciplined minds who are convinced that only the best will do in the strenuous race for the prizes of life, whether they be material, mental, or moral prizes. The man who, when he comes to do his work, is unable to find his tools, or to balance his figures, or to find the key of his desk, or the key to his thoughtless, will be struggling in his self made toils while his methodical neighbor will be freely and joyfully scaling the invigorating heights of successful achievement. The business man whose method is slovenly, or cumbersome, or behind the most recent developments of skilled minds, should only blame himself as his prospects are decadent, and should wake up to the necessity for more highly specialized and effective methods in his concern. He should seize upon every thing – every invention and idea – that will enable him to economize time and labour, and aid him in thoroughness, deliberation and dispatch.

System is the law by which everything – every organism, business, character, nation, empire – is built. By adding cell to cell, department to department, thought to thought, law to law, and colony to colony in orderly sequence and classification, all things, concerns and institutions grow in magnitude, and evolve to completeness. The man who is continually improving his methods, is gaining in building power; it therefore behoves the business man to be resourceful and inventive in the improvement of his methods, for the builders – whether of cathedrals or characters, business or religions – are the strong ones of the earth, and the protectors and pioneers of humanity. The systematic builder is a creator and preserver, while the man of disorder demolishes and destroys, and no limit can be set to the growth of a man's powers, the completeness of his character, the influence of his organization, or the extent of his business, if he but preserve intact the discipline of order, and have every detail in its place, keep every department to its special task, and tabulate and classify with such efficiency and perfection as to enable him at any moment to bring under examination or into requisition to the remotest detail in connection with his special work.

In system is contained these four ingredients:
1. Readiness
2. Reccuracy
3. Utility
4. Comprehensiveness

Readiness is aliveness. It is that spirit of alertness by which a situation is immediately grasped and dealt with. The observance of system fosters and develops this spirit. The successful General must have the power of readily meeting any new and unlooked for move on the part of the enemy; so every business man must have the readiness to deal with any unexpected develop-ment affecting his line of trade; and so also must the man of thought be able to deal with the details of any new problems which may arise. Dilatoriness is a vice that is fatal to prosperity, for it leads to incapability and stupidity. The men of ready hands, ready hearts, and ready brains, who know what they are doing, and do it methodically, skillfully, and with smooth yet consummate despatch are the men who need to think little of prosperity as an end, for it comes to them whether they seek it or not; success runs after them, and knocks at their door; and they unconsciously command it by the superb excellence of their faculties and methods.

Accuracy is of supreme importance in all commercial concerns and enterprises, but there can be no accuracy apart from system, and a system which is more or less imperfect will involve its originator in mistakes more or less disastrous until he improves it.

Inaccuracy is one of the commonest failings, because accuracy is closely allied to self-discipline, and self-discipline, along with that glad subjection to external discipline which it involves, is an indication of high moral culture to which the majority have not yet attained. If the inaccurate man will not willingly subject himself to the discipline of his employer or instructor, but thinks he knows better, his failing can never be remedied, and he will thereby bind himself down to an inferior position, if in the business world; or to imperfect knowledge, if in the world of thought.

The prevalence of the vice of inaccuracy (and in view of its disastrous effect it must be regarded as a vice, though perhaps one of the lesser vices) is patent to every observe in the way in which the majority of people relate a circumstance or repeat a simple statement of fact. It is nearly always made untrue by more or less marked inaccuracies. Few people, perhaps (not reckoning those who deliberately lie), have trained themselves to be accurate in what they say, or are so careful as to admit and state their liability to error, and from this common form of inaccuracy many untruths and misunderstand-ings arise.

More people take pains to be accurate in what they do than in what they say, but even here inaccuracy is very common, rendering many inefficient and incompetent, and unfitting them for any strenuous and well sustained endeavour. The man who habitually uses up a portion of his own or his employer's time in trying to correct his errors, or for the correction of whose mistakes another has to be employed, is not the man to maintain any position in the work a day world; much less to reach a place among the ranks of the prosperous.

There never yet lived a man who did not make some mistakes on his way to his particular success, but he is the capable and right minded man who perceives his mistakes and quickly remedies them, and who is glad when they are pointed out to him. It is habitual and persistent; inaccuracy which is a vice; and he is the incapable and wrong minded man who will not see or admit his mistakes, and who takes offence when they are pointed out to him.

The progressive man learns by his own mistakes as well as by the mistakes of others. He is always ready to test good advice by practice, and aims at greater and ever greater accuracy in his methods, which means higher and higher perfection, for accuracy is perfect, and the measure of a man's accuracy will be the measure of his uniqueness and perfection.

Utility or usefulness, is the direct result of method in one's work. Labour arrives at fruitful and profitable ends when it is systematically pursued. If the gardener is to gather in the best produce, he must not only sow and plant, but he must sow and plant at the right time; and if any work is to be fruitful in results, it must be done seasonably, and the time for doing a thing must not be allowed to pass by.

Utility considers the practical end; and employs the best means to reach that end. It avoids side issues, dispenses with theories, and retains its hold only on those things which can appropriated to good uses in the economy of life.

Unpractical people burden their minds with useless and unverifiable theories, and court failure by entertaining speculations which, by their very nature, cannot be applied in practice. The man whose powers are shown in what he does, and not in mere talking are arguing, avoids metaphysical quibbling and quandaries, and applies himself to the accomplishment of some good and useful end.

That which cannot be reduced to practice should not be allowed to hamper the mind. It should be thrown aside, abandoned, and ignored. A man recently told me that if his theory should be proved to have no useful end, he should still retain his hold upon it as a beautiful theory. If a man chooses to cling to so-called "beautiful" theories which are proved to have no use in life, and no substantial basis of reality, he must not be surprised if he fails in his wordly undertakings, for he is an unpractical man.

When the powers of the mind are diverted from speculative theorizing to practical doing, whether in material or moral directions, skill, power, knowledge, and prosperity increase. A man's prosperity is measured by his usefulness to the community, and a man is useful in accordance with that he does, and not because of the theories which he entertains.

The carpenter fashions a chair; the builder erects a house; the mechanic produces a machine; and the wise man moulds a perfect character. Not the schismatic, the theorists and the controversialists, but the workers, the makers, and the doers are the salt of the earth.

Let a man turn away from the mirages of intellectual speculation, and begin to do something, and to do it with all his might, and he will thereby gain a special knowledge, wield a special power, and reach his own unique position and prosperity among his fellows.

Comprehensiveness is that quality of mind which enables a man to deal with a large number of related details, to grasp them in their entirety, along with the single principle which governs them and binds them together. It is a masterly quality, giving organizing and governing power, and is developed by systematic attention to details. The successful merchant holds in his mind, as it were, all the details of his business, and regulates them by a system adapted to his particular form of trade. The inventor has in his mind all the details of his machine, along with their relation to a central mechanical principle, and so perfects his invention. The author of a great poem or story relates all his characters and incidents to a central plot, and so produces a composite and enduring literary work. Comprehensiveness is analytic and synthetic capacity combined in the same individual. A capacious and well ordered mind, which holds within its silent depths an army of details in their proper arrangement and true working order, is the mind that is near to genius, even if it has not already arrived. Every man cannot be a genius nor does he need to be, but he can be gradually evolving his mental capacity by careful attention to system in his thoughts and business, and as his intellect depends and broadens his powers will be intensified and his prosperity accentuated.

Such, then, are four corner pillars in the Temple of Prosperity, and of themselves they are sufficient to permanently sustain it without the addition of the remaining four. The man who perfects himself in Energy, Economy, Integrity, and System will achieve an enduring success in the work of his life, no matter what the nature of that work may be. It is impossible for one to fail who is full of energy, who carefully economizes his time and money, and virtuously husbands his vitality, who practices unswerving integrity, and who systematizes his work by first systematizing his mind.

Such a man's efforts will be rightly directed, and that, too, with concentrated power, so that they will be effective and fruitful. In addition he will reach a manliness and an independent dignity which will unconsciously command respect and success, and will strengthen weaker ones by its very presence in their midst. "Seest thou a man diligent in business; he shall stand before kings, he shall not stand before mean men," says Scripture of such a one. He will not beg, or whimper, or complain, or cynically blame others, but will be too strong and pure and upright a man to sink himself so low. And so standing high in the nobility and integrity of his character, he will fill a high place in the world and in the estimation of men. His success will be certain and his prosperity will endure. "He will stand and not fall in the battle of life."

Fifth Pillar – Sympathy

The remaining pillars are the four central pillars in the Temple of Prosperity. They gave it greater strength and stability, and add both to its beauty and utility. They contribute greatly to its attractiveness, for they belong to the highest moral sphere, and therefore to great beauty and nobility of character. They, indeed, make a man great, and place him among the comparatively few whose minds are rare, and that shine apart in sparkling purity and bright intelligence.

Sympathy should not be confounded with that maudlin and superficial sentiment which, like a pretty flower without root, presently perishes and leaves behind neither seed nor fruit. To fall into hysterical some suffering abroad, is not sympathy. Neither are bursts of violent indignation against the cruelties and injustices of others nor any indication of a sympathetic mind. If one is cruel at home – if he badgers his wife, or beats his children, or abuses his servants, or stabs his neighbors with shafts of bitter sarcasm what hypocrisy is in his profession of love for suffering people who are outside the immediate range of his influence! What shallow sentiment informs his bursts of indignation against the injustice and hard heartedness in the world around him.

Says Emerson of such – "Go, love they infant; love thy wood chopper; be good natured and modest; have that grace; and never varnish your hard uncharitable ambition with this incredible tenderness for black folk a thousand miles off. They love afar is spite at home." The test of a man is in his immediate acts, and not in ultra sentiments; and if those acts are consistently informed with selfishness and bitterness, if those at home hear his steps with dread, and feel a joyful relief on his departure, how empty are his expressions of sympathy for the suffering or down trodden how futile his membership of a philanthropic society.

Though the well of sympathy may feed the spring of tears, that spring more often draws its supply from the dark pool of selfishness, for when selfishness is thwarted it spends itself in tears.

Sympathy is a deep, silent, inexpressible tenderness which is shown in a consistently self forgetful gentle character. Sympathetic people are not gushing and spasmodic, but are permanently self restrained, firm, quiet, unassuming and gracious. Their undisturbed demeanour, where the suffering of others is concerned, is frequently mistaken for indifference by shallow minds, but the sympathetic and discerning eye recognizes, in their quiet strength and their swiftness to aid while others are sweeping, and wronging their hands, the deepest, soundest sympathy.

Lack of sympathy is shown in cynicism, illnatured sarcasm, bitter ridicule, taunting and mockery, and anger and condemnation, as well as in that morbid and false sentiment which is a theoretical and assumed sympathy, having no basis in practice.

Lack of sympathy arises in egotism; sympathy arises in love. Egotism is involved in ignorance; love is allied to knowledge. It is common with men to imagine themselves as separate from their fellows, with separate aims and interests; and to regard themselves as right and others wrong in their respective ways. Sympathy lifts a man above this separate and self centred life and enables him to live in the hearts of his fellows, and to think and feel with them. He puts himself in their place, and becomes, for the time being, as they are. As Whitman, the hospital hero, expresses it – "I do not ask the wounded person." It is a kind of impertinence to question a suffering creature. Suffering calls for aid and tenderness, and not for curiosity; and the sympathetic man or woman feels the suffering, and ministers to its alleviation.

Nor can sympathy boast, and wherever self praise enters in, sympathy passes out. If one speaks of his many deeds of kindness, and complains of the ill treatment he has received in return, he has not done kindly deeds, but has yet to reach that self forgetful modest which is the sweetness of sympathy.

Sympathy, in its real and profound sense, is oneness with others in their strivings and sufferings, so that the man of sympathy is a composite being; he is, as it were, a number of men, and he views a thing from a number of different sides, and not from one side only, and that his own particular side. He sees with the others men's eyes, hears with their ears, thinks with their minds, and feels with their hearts. He is thus able to understand men who are vastly different from himself; the meaning of their lives is revealed to him, and he is united to them in the spirit of goodwill. Said Balzac – "The poor fascinate me; their hunger is my hunger; I am with them in their homes; their privations I suffer; I feel the beggar's rags upon my back; I for the time being become the poor and despised man." It reminds us of the saying of One greater than Balzac, that a deed done for a suffering little one was done for him.

And so it is; sympathy leads us to the hearts of all men, so that we become spiritually united to them, and when they suffer we feel the pain; when they are glad we rejoice with them; when they are despised and persecuted, we spiritually descend with them into the depths, and take into our hearts their humiliation and distress; and he who has this binding, uniting spirit of sympathy, can never be cynical and condemnatory can never pass thoughtless and cruel judgements upon his fellows; because in his tenderness of heart he is ever with them in their pain.

But to have reached this ripened sympathy, it must needs be that one has loved much, suffered much and sounded the dark depths of sorrow. It springs from acquaintance with the profoundest experiences, so that a man has ad conceit, thoughtlessness, and selfishness burnt out of his heart. No man can have true sympathy who has not been, in some measure at least, "a man of sorrows, and acquainted with grief," but the sorrow and grief must have passed, must have ripened into a fixed kindness and habitual calm.

To have suffered so much in a certain direction that the suffering is finished, and only its particular wisdom remains, enables one, wherever that suffering presents itself, to understand and deal with it by pure sympathy; and when one has been "perfected by suffering" in many directions, he becomes a centre of rest and healing for the sorrowing and broken hearted who are afflicted with the affections which he has experienced and conquered. As a mother feels the anguish of her suffering child, so the man of sympathy feels the anguish of suffering men.

Such is the highest and holiest sympathy, but a sympathy much less perfect is a great power for good in human life and a measure of it is everywhere and every day needed. While rejoicing in the fact that in every walk in life there are truly sympathetic people, one also perceives that harshness, resentment, and cruelty are all too common. These hard qualities bring their own sufferings, and there are those who fail in their business, or particular work, entirely because of the harshness of their disposition. A man who is fiery and resentful, or who is hard, cold and calculating, with the springs of sympathy dried up within him, even though he be otherwise an able man, will, in the end scarcely avoid disaster in his affairs. His heated folly in the one case, or cold cruelty in the other, will gradually isolate him from his fellows and from those who are immediately related to him in his particular avocation, so that the elements of prosperity will be eliminated from his life, leaving him with a lonely failure, and perhaps a hopeless despair.

Even in ordinary business transactions, sympathy is an important factor, for people will always be attracted to those who are of a kindly and genial nature, preferring to deal with them rather than with those who are hard and forbidding. In all spheres where direct personal contact plays an important part, the sympathetic man with average ability will always take precedence of the man of greater ability but who is unsympathetic.

If a man be a minister or a clergyman, a cruel laugh or an unkind sentence from him will seriously injure his reputation and influence, but particularly his influence, for even they who admire his good qualities will, through his unkindness, unconsciously have a lower regard for him in their personal esteem.

If a business man profess religion, people will expect to see the good influence of that religion on his business transactions. To profess to be a worshipper of the gentle Jesus on Sunday, and all the rest of the wee be a hard, grasping worshipper of mammon, will injure his trade, and detract considerably from his prosperity.

Sympathy is a universal spiritual language which all, even the animals, instinctively understand and appreciate, for all beings and creatures are subject to suffering, and this sameness of painful experience leads to that unity of feeling which we call sympathy.

Selfishness impels men to protect themselves at the expense of others; but sympathy impels them to protect others by the sacrifice of self; and in this sacrifice of self there is no real and ultimate loss, for while the pleasure of selfishness are small and few, the blessings of sympathy are great and manifold.

It may be asked, "How can a business man; whose object is to develop his own trade, practice self-sacrifice?" Even man can practice self sacrifice just where he is, and in the measure that he is capable of understand it. If one contends that he cannot practice a virtue it, for were his circumstances different, he would still have the same excuse. Diligence in business is not incompatible with self sacrifice, for devotion to duty, even though that duty be trade, is not selfishness, but may be an unselfish devotion. I know a business man who, when a competitor who had tried to 'cut him out' in business, cut himself out and failed, set that same competitor up in business again. Truly a beautiful act of self sacrifice; and the man that did it is, today, one of the most successful and prosperous of business men.

The most prosperous commercial traveler I have ever known, was overflowing with exuberant kindness and geniality. He was as innocent of all "tricks of trade" as a new born infant, but his great heart and manly uprightness won for him fast friends wherever he went. Men were glad to see him come into their office or shop or mill, and not alone for the good and bracing influence he brought with him, but also because his business was sound and trustworthy. This man was successful through sheer sympathy, but sympathy so pure and free from policy, that he himself would probably have denied that his success could be attributed to it. Sympathy can never hinder success. It is selfishness that blights and destroys. As goodwill increases, man's prosperity will increase. All interests are mutual, and stand or fall together, and as sympathy expands the heart, it extends the circle of influence, making blessings, both spiritual and material, to more greatly abound.

Fourfold are the qualities which make up the great virtue of sympathy, namely:—

1. Kindness
2. Generosity
3. Gentleness
4. Insight

Kindness, when fully developed, is not a passing impulse but a permanent quality. An intermittent and unreliable impulse is not kindness, though it often goes under that name. There is no kindness in praise if it be followed by abuse. The love which seems to prompt the spontaneous kiss will be of little account if it be associated with a spontaneous spite. The gift which seemed so gracious will lose its value should the giver afterwards wish its value in return. To have one's feelings aroused to do a kind action towards another by some external stimulus pleasing to one's self, and shortly afterwards to be swayed to the other extreme towards the same person by an external event unpleasing to one's self, should be regarded as weakness of character; and it is also a selfish condition, us, and when he pleases us, to be thinking of one's self only. A true kindness is unchangeable, and needs no external stimulus to force it into action. It is a well from which thirsty souls can always drink, and it never runs dry. Kindness, when it is a strong virtue, is bestowed not only on those who please us, but also upon those whose actions go contrary to our wish and will, and it is a constant and never – varying glow of genial warmth.

There are some actions of which men repent; such are all unkind actions. There are other actions of which men do not repent, and such are all kind actions. The day comes when men are sorry for the cruel things they said and did; but the day of gladness is always with them for the kindly things they have said and done.

Unkindness mars a man's character, it mars his face as time goes on, and it mars that perfection of success which he would otherwise reach.

Kindness beautifies the character, it beautifies the face with the growth of the years, and it enables a man to reach that perfection of success to which his intellectual abilities entitle him. A man's prosperity is mellowed and enriched by the kindness of his disposition.

Generosity goes with a larger hearted kindness. If kindness be the gentle sister, Generosity is the strong brother. A free, open handed, and magnanimous character is always attractive and influential. Stringiness and meanness always repel; they are dark, cramped, narrow, and cold. Kindness and generosity always attack; they are sunny, genial, open, and warm. That which repels makes for isolation and failure; that which attracts makes for union and success.

Giving is as important a duty as getting; and he who gets all he can, and refuses to give, will at last be unable to get; for it is as much a spiritual law that we cannot get unless we give, as that we cannot give unless we get.

Giving has always been taught as a great and important duty by all the religious teachers. This is because giving is one of the highways of personal growth and progress. It is a means by which we attain to greater and greater unselfishness, and by which we prevent the falling back into selfishness. It implies that we recognize our spiritual and social kinship with our fellow-men, and are willing to part with a portion of that we have earned or possess, for man who, the more he gets, hungers for more still, and refuses to loosen his grasp upon his accumulating store, like a wild beast with its prey, is retrogressing; he is shutting himself out from all the higher and joy giving qualities, and from free and life giving communion with unselfish, happy human hearts. Dickens's Scrooge in "A Christmas Carol" represents the condition of such a man with graphic vividness and dramatic force.

Our public men in England to-day (probably also in America) are nearly all (I think I might say all, for I have not yet met an exception) great givers. These men – Lord Mayors, Mayors, Magistrates, Town and City Councillors, and all men filling responsible public offices – being men who have been singularly successful in the management of their own private affairs, are considered the best men for the management of public affairs, and numerous noble institutions throughout the land are perpetual witnesses to the munificence of their gifts. Nor have I been able to find any substantial truth in the accusation, so often hurled against such men by the envious and unsuccessful, that their riches are made unjustly. Without being perfect men, they are an honourable class of manly, vigorous, generous, and successful men, who have acquired riches and honour by sheer industry, ability and uprightness.

Let a man beware of greed, of meanness, of envy, of jealousy, of suspicion, for these things, if harboured, will rob him of all that is best in life, aye, even all that is best in material things, as well as all that is best in character and happiness. Let him be liberal of heart and generous of hand, magnanimous and trusting, not only giving cheerfully and often of his substance, but allowing his friends and fellow-men freedom of thought and action – let him be thus, and honour, plenty, and prosperity will come knocking at the door for admittance as his friends and guests.

Gentleness is akin to divinity. Perhaps no quality is so far removed from all that is coarse, brutal and selfish as gentleness, so that when one is becoming gentle, he is becoming divine. It can only be acquired after much experience and through great self-discipline. It only becomes established in a man's heart when he has controlled and brought into subjection his animal voice, a distinct, firm, but quiet enunciation, and freedom from excitement, vehemence, or resentment in peculiarly aggravating circumstances.

If there is one quality which, above all others, should distinguish the religious man, it is the quality of gentleness, for it is the hall mark of spiritual culture. The rudely aggressive man is an affront to cultivated minds and unselfish hearts. Our word gentlemen has not altogether departed from its original meaning. It is still applied to one who is modest and self-restrained, and is considerate for the feelings and welfare of others. A gentle man one whose good behavior is prompted by thoughtfulness and kindliness is always loved, whatever may be his origin. Quarrelsome people make a display in their bickering and recriminations – of their ignorance and lack of culture. The man who has perfected himself in gentleness never quarrels. He never returns the hard word; he leaves it alone, or meets it with a gentle word which is far more powerful than wrath. Gentleness is wedded to wisdom, and the wise man has overcome all anger in himself, and so understands how to overcome it in others. The gentleman is saved from most of the disturbances and turmoil's with which uncontrolled men afflict themselves. While they are wearing themselves out with wasteful and needless strain, he is quiet and composed, and such quietness and composure are strong to win in the battle of life.

Insight is the gift of sympathy. The sympathetic mind is the profoundly perceiving mind. We understand by experience, and not by argument. Before we can know a thing or being, our life must touch its or his life. Argument analyzes the outer skin, but sympathy reaches to the heart. The cynic sees the hat and coat, and thinks he sees the man. The sympathetic seer sees the man, and is not concerned with the hat and coat. In all kinds of hatred there is a separation by which each misjudges the other. In all kinds of love there is a mystic union by which each knows the other. Sympathy, being the purest form of this the greatest poet because he has the largest heart. No other figure in all literature has shown such a profound knowledge of the human heart, and of nature both animate and inanimate. The personal Shakespeare is not to be found in his works; he is merged, by sympathy, into his characters. The wise man and the philosopher; the madman and the fool; the drunkard and the harlot – these he, for the time into their particular experiences and knew them better than they knew themselves. Shakespeare has no partiality, no prejudice; his sympathy embraces all, from the lowest to the highest.

Prejudice is the great barrier to sympathy and knowledge. It is impossible to understand those against whom one harbours a prejudice. We only see men and things as they are when we divest our minds of partial judgements. We become seers as we become sympathizers. Sympathy has knowledge for her companion.

Inseparable are the feeling heart and the seeing eye. The man of pity is the man of prophecy. He whose heart beats in tune with all hearts, to him the contents of all hearts are revealed. Nor are past and future any longer insoluble mysteries to the man of sympathy. His moral insight apprehends the perfect round of human life.

Sympathetic insight lifts a man into the consciousness of freedom, gladness and power. His spirit inhales joy as his lungs inhale air. There are no longer any fears of his fellow-men of competition, hard times, enemies, and the like. These grovelling illusion have disappeared, and there has opened up before his awakened vision a realm of greatness and grandeur.

Sixth Pillar – Sincerity

Human society is held together by its sincerity. A universal falseness would beget a universal mistrust which would bring about a universal separation, if not destruction. Life is made sane, wholesome, and happy, by our deep rooted belief in one another. If we did not trust men, we could not transact business with them, could not even associate with them. Shakespeare's "Timon" shows us the wretched condition of a man who, through his own folly, has lost all faith in the sincerity of human nature. He cuts himself off from the company of all men, and finally commits suicide. Emerson has something to the effect that if the trust system were withdrawn from commerce, society would fall to pieces; that system being an indication of the universal confidence men place in each other. Business, commonly supposed by the shortsighted and foolish to be all fraud and deception is based on a great trust – a trust that men will meet and fulfil their obligations. Payment is not asked until the goods are delivered; and the fact of the continuance of this system for ages, proves that most men do pay their debts, and have no wish to avoid such payment.

Back of all its shortcomings, human society rests on a strong basis of truth. Its fundamental note in sincerity. Its great leaders are all men of superlative sincerity; and their names and achievements are not allowed to perish – a proof that the virtue of sincerity is admired by all the race.

It is easy for the insincere to imagine that everybody is like themselves, and to speak of the "rottenness of society," — though a rotten thing could endure age after age, for is not everything yellow to the jaundiced eye? People who cannot see anything good in the constitution of human society, should overhaul themselves. Their trouble is near home. They call good, evil. They have dwelt cynically and peevishly on evil till they cannot see good, and everything and everybody appears evil. "Society is rotten from top to bottom," I heard a man say recently; and he asked me if I did not think so. I replied that I should be sorry to think so; that while society had many blemishes, it was sound at the core, and contained within itself the seeds of perfection.

Society, indeed is so sound that the man who is playing a part for the accomplishment of entirely selfish ends cannot long prosper, and cannot fill any place as an influence. He is soon unmasked and disagreed; and the fact that such a man can, for even a brief period, batten on human credulity, speaks well for the trustfulness of men, if it reveals their lack of wisdom.

An accomplished actor on the stage is admired, but the designing actor on the stage of life brings himself down to ignominy and contempt. In striving to appear what he is not, he becomes as one having no individuality, no character, and he is deprived of all influence, all power, all success.

A man of profound sincerity is a great moral force, and there is no force – not even the highest intellectual force – that can compare with it. Men are powerful in influence according to the soundness and perfection of their sincerity. Morality and sincerity are so closely bound up together, that where sincerity is lacking, morality, as a power, is lacking also, for insincerity undermines all the other virtues, so that they crumble away and become of no account. Even a little insincerity robs a character of all its nobility, and makes it common and contemptible. Falseness is so despicable a vice and no man of moral weight can afford to dally with pretty complements, or play the fool with trivial and howsoever light, in order to please, and he is no longer strong and admirable, but is become a shallow weakling whose mind has no deep well of power from which men can draw, and no satisfying richness to stir in them a worshipful regard.

Even they who are for the moment flattered with the painted lie, or pleased with the deftly woven deception, will not escape those permanent under currents of influence which move the heart and shape the judgement to fixed and final issues, while these designed delusions create but momentary ripples on the surface of the mind.

"I am very pleased with his attentions," said a woman of an acquaintance, "but I would not marry him." "Why not?" she was asked. "He doesn't ring true," was the reply.

Ring true, a term full of meaning. It has reference to the coin which, when tested by its ring, emits a sound which reveals the sterling metal throughout, without the admixture of any base material. It comes up to the standard, and will pass anywhere and everywhere for its full value.

So with men. Their words and actions emit their own peculiar influence. There is in them an inaudible sound which all other men inwardly hear and instinctively detect. They know the false ring from the true, yet know not how they know. As the outer ear can make the most delicate distinctions in sounds, so the inner ear can make equally subtle distinctions between souls. None are ultimately deceived but the deceiver. It is the blind folly of the insincere that, while flattering themselves upon their successful simulations, they are deceiving none but themselves. Their actions are laid bare before all hearts. There is at the hear of man a tribunal whose judgements do not miscarry. If the senses faultlessly detect, shall not the soul infallibly know! This inner infallibility is shown in the collective judgement of the race. This judgement is perfect; so perfect than in literature, art, science, invention, religion – in every department of knowledge – it divides the good from the bad, the worthy from the unworthy, the true from the false, zealously guarding and preserving the former, and allowing the latter to perish. The works, words, and deeds of great men are the heirlooms of the race, and the race is not careless of their value. A thousand men write a book, and one only is a work of original genius, yet the race singles out that one, elevates and preserves it, while it consigns the nine hundred and ninety nine copyists to oblivion. Ten thousand men utter a sentence under a similar circumstance, and one only is a sentence of divine wisdom, yet the race singles out that saying for the guidance of posterity, while the other sentences are heard no more. It is true that the race slays its prophets, but even that slaying becomes a test which reveals the true ring, and men detect its tureens. The slain one has come up to the standard, and the deed of his slaying is preserved as furnishing infallible proof of his greatness.

As the counterfeit coin is detected, and cast back into the melting pot, while the sterling coin circulates among all men, and is valued for its worth, so the counterfeit word, deed, or character is perceived, and is left to fall back into the nothingness from which it emerged, a thing unreal, powerless, dead.

Spurious things have no value, whether they be bric-a-brac or men. We are ashamed of imitations that try to pass for the genuine article. Falseness is cheap. The masquerader becomes a byword; he is less than a man; he is a shadow, a spook, a mere mask. Trueness is valuable. The sound hearted man becomes an exemplar; he is more than a man; he is a reality; a force, a moulding principle, by falseness all is lost – even individuality dissolves for falseness is nonentity, nothingness. By trueness everything is gained, for trueness is fixed, permanent, real.

It is all important that we be real; that we harbour no wish to appear other than what we are; that we simulate no virtue, assume no excellency, adopt no disguise. The hypocrite thinks he can hood wink the world and the eternal law of the world. There is but one person that he hoodwinks, and that is himself, and for that the law of the world inflicts its righteous penalty. There is an old theory that the excessively wicked are annihilated. I think to be a pretender is to come as near to annihilation as a man can get, for there is a sense in which the man is gone, and in his place there is but a mirage of shams. The hell of annihilation which so many dread, he has descended into; and to think that such a man can prosper is to think that shadows can do the work of entities, and displace real men.

If any man thinks he can build up a successful career on pretences and appearances, let him pause before sinking into the abyss of shadows; for in insincerity there is no solid ground, no substance, no reality; there is nothing on which anything can stand, and no material with which to build; but there are loneliness, poverty, shame, confusion, fears, suspicions, weeping, groaning, and lamentations; for if there is one hell lower, darker, fouler than all others, it is the hell of insincerity.

Four beautiful traits adorn the mind of the sincere man; they are:—

1. Simplicity
2. Attractiveness
3. Penetration
4. Power

Simplicity is naturalness. It is simple being, without fake or foreign adornment. Why are all things in nature so beautiful? Because they are natural. We see them as they are, no task they might wish to appear, for in sooth they have no wish to appear, for in sooth they have no wish to appear otherwise. There is no hypocrisy in the world of nature outside of human nature. The flower which is so beautiful in all eyes would lose its beautify in all eyes would nature we look upon reality, and its beauty and perfection gladden and amaze us. We cannot find anywhere a flaw, and are conscious of our incapacity to improve upon anything, even to the most insignificant. Everything ha sits own peculiar perfection, and shines in the beauty of unconscious simplicity.

One of the modern social cries is, "Back to nature." It is generally understood to mean a cottage in the country, and a piece of land to cultivate. It will be of little use to go into the country if we take our shams with us; and any veneer which may cling to us can as well be washed off just where we are. It is good that they who feel burdened with the conventions of society should fly to the country, and court the quiet of nature, but it will fail if it by anything but a means to that inward redemption which will restore us to the simple and the true.

But though humanity has wandered from the natural simplicity of the animal world, it is moving towards a higher, a divine simplicity. Men of great genius are such because of their spontaneous simplicity. They do not foreign; they are. Lesser minds study style and effect. They wish to cut a striking figure on the stage of the world, and by that unholy wish they are doomed to mediocrity. Said a man to me recently, "I would give twenty years of my life to be able to write an immortal hymn." With such an ambition a man cannot write a hymn. He wants to pose. He is thinking of himself, of his own glory. Before a man can writer an immortal hymn, or create any immortal work he must give, not twenty years of his life to ambition but his can do anything great, and must sing, paint, write, out of ten thousand bitter experiences, ten thousand failures, ten thousand conquests, ten thousand joys. He must know Gethsemane; he must work with blood and tears.

Retaining his intellect and moral powers, and returning to simplicity, a man becomes great. He forfeits nothing real. Only the shams are cast aside, revealing the standard gold of character. Where there is sincerity there will always be simplicity – a simplicity of the kind that we see in nature, the beautiful simplicity of truth.

Attractiveness is the direct outcome of simplicity. This is seen in the attractiveness of all natural objects; to which we have referred, but in human nature it is manifested as personal influence. Of recent years certain pseudomystics have been advertising to sell the secret of "personal magne-tism" for so many dollars, by which they purport to show vain people how they can make themselves attractive to others by certain "occult" means as though attractiveness can be brought and sold, and put on and off like powder and paint. Nor are people who are anxious to be thought attractive, likely to become so, for their vanity is a barrier to it. The very desire to be thought attractive is, in itself, a deception, and it leads to the practice of numerous deceptions. It infers, too, that such people are conscious of lacking the genuine attractions and graces of character, and are on the look out for a substitute; but there is no substitute for beauty of mind and strength of character. Attractiveness, like genius, is lost by being coveted, and possessed by those who are too solid and sincere of character to desire it. There is nothing in human nature – nor talent, nor intellect, nor affection, nor beauty of features that can compare in attractive power with that soundness of mind and wholeness of heart which we call sincerity. There is a perennial charm about a sincere man or woman, and they draw about themselves the best specimens of human nature. There can be no personal charm apart from sincerity. Infatuation there may be, and is, but this is a kind of disease, and is vastly different from the indissoluble bond by which sincere people are attached. Infatuation ends in painful disillusion, but as there is nothing hidden between sincere souls, and they stand upon that solid ground of reality, there is no illusion to be displayed.

Leaders among men attract by the power of their sincerity, and the measures of their sincerity is the measure of their sincerity is the great may be a man's intellect he can never be a permanent leader and guide of men unless he be sincere. For a time he may sail jauntily upon the stream of popularity, and believe himself secure, but it is only that he may shortly fall the lower in popular odium. He cannot long deceive the people with his painted front. They will soon look behind, and find of what spurious stuff he is made. He is like a woman with a painted face. She thinks she is admired for her complexion, but all know it is paint, and despise her for it. she has one admirer – herself, and the hell of limitation to which all the insincere commit themselves is the hell of self admiration.

Sincere people do not think of themselves, of their talent, their genius, their virtue, their beautify and because they are so unconscious of themselves, they attract all, and win their confidence, affection, and esteem.

Penetration belongs to the sincere. All shams are unveiled in their presence. All simulators are transparent to the searching eye of the sincere man. With one clear glance he sees through all their flimsy pretences. Tricksters with under his strong gaze, and want to get away from it. He who has rid his heart of all falseness, and entertains only that which is true, has gained the power to distinguish the false from the true in others. He is not deceived who is not self deceived.

As men, looking around on the objects of nature, infallibly distinguish them such as a snake, a bird, a horse, a tree, a rose, and so on – so the sincere man distinguishes between the variety of characters. He perceives in a movement, a look, a word, an act, the nature of the man, and acts accordingly. He is on his guard without being suspicious. He is prepared for the pretender without being mistrustful. He acts from positive knowledge, and not from negative suspicion. Men are open to him, and he reads their contents. His penetrative judgement pierces to the centre of actions. His direct and unequivocal conduct strengthens in others the good, and shames the bad, and he is a staff of strength to those who have not yet attained to his soundness of heart and head.

Power goes with penetration. An understanding of the nature of actions is accompanied with the power to meet and deal with all actions in the right and best way. Knowledge is always power, but knowledge of the nature of actions is superlative power, and he who possesses it becomes a Presence to all hearts, and modifies their actions for good. Long after his bodily presence has passed away, he is still a moulding force in the world and is a spiritual reality working subtly in the minds of men, and shaping them towards sublime ends. At first his power local and limited, but the circle of righteousness which he has set moving, continues to extend and extended till it embraces the whole world, and all men are influenced by it.

The sincere man stamps his character upon all that he does, and also upon all people with whom he comes in contact. He speaks a word in season, and some one is impressed; the influence is communicated to another, and another, and presently some despairing soul ten thousand miles away hears it and is restored. Such a power is prosperity in itself, and its worth is not to be valued in coin. Money cannot purchase the priceless jewels of character, but labour in right doing can, and he who makes himself sincere, who acquires a robust soundness throughout his entire being, will become a man of singular success and rare power.

Such is the strong pillar of sincerity. It supporting power is to great that, one it is completely erected, the Temple of Prosperity is secure. Its walls will not crumble; its rafters will not decay; its roof will not fall in. It will stand while the man lives, and when has passed away it will continue to afford a shelter and a home for others through many generation.

Seventh Pillar – Impartiality

To get rid of prejudice is a great achievement. Prejudices piles obstacles in a man's way – obstacles to health, success, happiness, and prosperity, so that he is continually running up against imaginary enemies, who, when prejudice is removed, are seen to be friend. Life, indeed, a sort of obstacle race to the man of prejudice, a race wherein the obstacles cannot be negotiated and the goal is not reached; whereas to the impartial man life is a day's walk in a pleasant country, with refreshment and rest at the end of the day.

To acquire impartiality, a man must remove that innate egotism which prevents him from seeing any thing from any point of view other than this own. A great task, truly; but a notable, and one that can be well begun now, even if it cannot be finished. Truth can "remove mountains," and prejudice is a range of mental mountains beyond which the partisan does not see, and of which he does not believe there is any beyond. These mountains removed, however, there opens to the view the unending vista of mental variety blended in one glorious picture of light and shade, of colour and tone, gladdening beholding eyes.

By clinging to stubborn prejudice what joys are missed, what friends are sacrificed, what happiness is destroyed, and what prospects are blighted! And yet freedom from prejudice is a rare thing. There are few men who are not prejudiced partisans upon the subjects which are of interest to them. One rarely meets a man that will dispassionately discuss his subject from both sides, considering all the facts and weighing all the evidence so as to arrive at truth on the matter. Each partisan has his own case to make out. He is not searching for truth, for he is already convinced that his own conclusion is the truth, and that all else is error; but he is defending his own case, and striving for victory. Neither does he attempt to prove that he has the truth by a calm array of facts and evidence, but defends his position with more or less heat and agitation.

Prejudice causes a man to form a conclusion, sometimes without any basis of fact or knowledge, and then to refuse to consider anything which does not support that conclusion; and in this way prejudice is a complete barrier to the attainment of knowledge. It binds a man down to darkness and ignorance, and prevents the development of his mind in the highest and noblest directions. More than this, it also shuts him out from communion with the best minds, and confines him to the dark and solitary cell of his own egotism.

Prejudice is a shutting up of the mind against the entrance of new light, against the perception of more beauty, against the hearing of diviner music. The partisan clings to his little, fleeting, flimsy opinion, and thinks it the greatest thing in the world. He is so in love with his own conclusion (which is only a form of self love), that he thinks all men ought to agree with him, and he regards men as more or less stupid who do not see as he sees, while he praises the good judgement of those who are one with him in his view. Such a man cannot have knowledge, cannot have truth. He is confined to the sphere of opinion (to his own self created illusions) which is outside the realm of reality. He moves in a kind of self infatuation which prevents him from seeing the commonest facts of life, while his own theories – usually more or less groundless – assume, in his mind, overpowering proportions. He fondly imagines that there is but one side to everything, and that side is his own. There are at least two sides to everything, and he it is who finds the truth in a matter who carefully examines both sides with all freedom from excitement, and without any desire for the predominance of one side over another.

In its divisions and controversies the world at large is like two lawyers defending a case. The counsel for the prosecution presents all the facts which prove his side, while counsel for the defense presents all the facts which support his contention, and each belittles or ignores, or tries to reason away, the facts of the other. The Judge in the case, however, is like the impartial thinker among men: having listened to all the evidence on both sides, he compares and sifts it so as to form an impartial summing up in the cause of justice.

Not that this universal partiality is a bad thing, nor as in all other extremes, nature here reduces the oppositions of conflicting parties to a perfect balance; moreover, it is a factor in evolution; it stimulates men to think who have not yet developed the power to rouse up vigorous thought at will, and it is a phase through which all men have to pass. But it is only byway – and a tangled, confused and painful one – towards the great highway of Truth. It is the are of which impartiality is the perfect round. The partisan sees a portion of the truth, and thinks it the whole, but the impartial thinker sees the whole truth which includes all sides. It is necessary that we find see truth in sections, as it were, until, having gathered up all the parts, we may piece them together and form the perfect circle, and the forming of such circle is the attainment of impartiality.

The impartial man examines, weighs, and considers, with freedom from prejudice and from likes and dislikes. His one wish is to discover the truth. He abolishes preconceived opinions, and lets facts and evidence speak for themselves. He has no case to make out for himself, for he knows that truth is unalterable, that his opinions can make no difference to it, and that it can be investigated and discovered. He thereby escapes a vast amount of friction and nervous wear and tear to which the feverish partisan is subject; and in addition, he looks directly upon the face of Reality, and so becomes tranquil and peaceful.

So rare is freedom from prejudice that wherever the impartial thinker may be, he is sure, sooner or later, to occupy a very high position in the estimation of the world, and in the guidance of its destiny. Not necessarily an office in worldly affairs, for that is improbable, but an exalted position in the sphere of influence. There may be such a one now, and he may be a carpenter, a weaver, a clerk; he may be in poverty or in the home of a millionaire; he may be short or tall, or of any complexion, but whatever and wherever he may be, he has, though unknown, already begun to move the world, and will one day be universally recognized at a new force and creative centre in evolution.

There was one such some nineteen hundred years ago. He was only a poor, unlettered carpenter; He was regarded as a madman by His own relatives, and he came to an ignominious end in the eyes of His countrymen, but He sowed the seeds of an influence which has altered the whole world.

There was another such in India some twenty five centuries ago. He was accomplished, highly educated, and was the son of a capitalist and landed proprietor a petty king. He became a penniless, homeless mendicant, and to day one third of the human race worship at his shrine, and are restrained and elevated by his influence.

"Beware when the great God lets loose a thinker on this plane," says Emerson; and a man is not a thinker who is bound by prejudice; he is merely the strenuous upholder of an opinion. Every idea must pass through the medium of his particular prejudice, and receive its colour, so that dispassion-ate thinking and impartial judgement are rendered impossible. Such a man sees everything only in its relation, or imagined relation, to his opinion, whereas the thinker sees things as they are. The man who has so purified his mind of prejudice and of all the imperfections of egotism as to be able to look directly upon reality, has reached the acme of power; he holds in his hands, as it were, the vastest influence, and he will wield this power whether he knows it or not; it will be inseparable from his life, and will go from him as perfume from the flower. It will be in his words, his deeds, in his bodily postures and the motions of his mind, even in his silence and the stillness of his frame. Wherever he goes, even though he should fly to the desert, he will not escape this lofty destiny, for a great thinker is the centre of the world; by him all men are held in their orbits and all thought gravitates towards him.

The true thinker lives above and beyond the seething whirlpool of passion in which mankind is engulfed. He is not swayed by personal consideration, for he has grasped the importance of impersonal principles, and being thus a noncombatant in the clashing warfare of egotistic desires, he can, from the vantage ground of an impartial but not indifferent watcher, see both sides equally, and grasp the cause and meaning of the fray.

Not only the Great Teachers, but the greatest figures in literature, are those who are free from prejudice, who, like true mirrors, effect things impartially. Such are Whitman, Shakespeare, Balzac, Emerson, Homer. These minds are not local, but universal. Their attitude is cosmic and not personal.

They contain within themselves all things and beings all worlds and laws. They are the gods who guide the race, and who will bring it at last out of its fever of passion into their own serene land.

The true thinker is the greatest of men, and his destiny is the most exalted. The altogether impartial mind has reached the divine, and it basks in the full daylight of Reality.

The four great elements of impartiality are

1. Justice
2. Patience
3. Calmness
4. Wisdom

Justice is the giving and receiving of equal values. What is called "striking a hard bargain" is a kind of theft. It means that the purchaser gives value for only a portion of his purchase, the remainder being appropriated as clear gain. The seller also encourages it by closing the bargain.

The just man does not try to gain an advantage; he considers the true values of things, and moulds his transactions in accordance therewith. He does not let "what will pay" come before "what is right," for he knows that the right pays best in the end. He does not seek his own benefit to the disadvantage of another, for he knows that a just action benefits, equally and fully, both parties to a transaction. If "one man's loss is another man's gain," it is only that the balance may be adjusted later on. Unjust gains cannot lead to prosperity, but are sure to bring failure. A just man could no more take from another an unjust gain by what is called a "smart transaction" that he could take it by picking his pocket. He would regard the one as dishonest as the other.

The bargaining spirit in business is not the true spirit of commerce. It is the selfish and thieving spirit which wants to get something for nothing. The upright man purges his business of all bargaining, and builds it one the more dignified basis of justice. He supplies "a good article" at its right price, and does not alter. He does not soil his hands with any business which is tainted with fraud. His goods are genuine and they are properly priced.

Customers who try to "beat down" a tradesman in their purchases are degrading themselves. Their practice assumes one or both of two things, namely, that either the tradesman is dishonest and is overcharging (a low, suspicious attitude of mind), or that they are eager to cajole him out of his profit (an equally base attitude), and so benefit by his loss. The practice of "bearing down" is altogether a dishonest one, and the people who pursue it most assiduously are those who complain most of being "imposed on" and this is not surprising, seeing that they themselves are all the time trying to impose upon others.

On the other hand, the tradesman who is anxious to get all he can out of his customers, irrespective of justice and the right values of things, is a kind of robber, and is slowly poisoning his success, for his deeds will assuredly come home to him in the form of financial ruin.

Said a man of fifty to me other day, "I have just discovered that all my life I have been paying fifty percent, more for everything than I ought to." A just man cannot feel that he has ever paid too much for anything, for he does not close with any transaction which he considers unjust; but if a man is eager to get everything at half price, them he will be always meanly and miserably mourning that he is paying double for everything. The just man is glad to pay full value for everything, whether in giving or receiving and his mind is untroubled and his days are full of peace.

Let a man above all avoid meanness, and strive to be ever more and more perfectly just, for if not just, he can be neither honest, nor generous, nor manly, but is a kind of disguised thief trying to get all he can, and give back as little as possible. Et him eschew all bargaining, and teach bargainers a better way by conducting his business with that exalted dignity which commands a large and meritorious success.

Patience is the brightest jewel in the character of the impartial man. Not a particular patience with a particular thing – like a girl with her needlework, or a boy building his toy engine but on unswerving considerateness, a sweetness of disposition at all times and under the most trying circumstances, an unchangeable and gentle strength which no trial can mar and no persecution can break. A rare possession, it is true, and one not to be expected for a long time yet from the bulk of mankind, but a virtue that can be reached by degree, and even a partial patience will work wonders in a man's life and affairs, as a confirmed impatience all work devastation. The irascible man is courting speedy disaster, for who will care to deal with a man who continually going off like ground powder when some small spark of complaint or criticism falls upon him! Even his friends will one by one desert him, for who would court the company of a man who rudely assaults him with an impatient and fiery tongue over every little difference or misunderstanding.

A man must begin to wisely control himself, and to learn the beautiful lessons of patience, if he is to be highly prosperous, if he is to be a man of use and power. He must learn to think of others, to act for their good, and not alone for himself; to be considerate, for bearing, and long suffering. He must study how to have a heart at peace with men who differ from him on those things which he regards as most vital. He must avoid quarrelling as he would avoid drinking a deadly poison. Discords from without will be continually overtaking him, but he must fortify himself against them; he must study how to bring harmonies out of them by the exercise of patience.

Strife is common: it pains the heart and distorts the mind. Patience is rare, it enriches the heart and beautifies the mind. Every cat can spit and fume; it requires no effort, but only a looseness of behavior. It takes a man to keep his mornings through all events, and to be painstaking and patient with the shortcomings of humanity. But patience wins. As soft water wears away the hardest rock, so patience overcomes all opposition. It gains the hearts of men. It conquers and controls.

Calmness accompanies patience. It is a great and glorious quality. It is the peaceful haven of emancipated souls after their long wanderings on the tempest riven ocean of passion. It makes the man who has suffered much, endured much, experienced much, and has finally conquered.

A man cannot be impartial who is not calm. Excitement, prejudice, and partiality spring from disturbed passions. When personal feeling is thwarted, it rises and seethes like a stream of water that is dammed. The calm man avoids this disturbance by directing his feeling from the personal to the impersonal channel. He thinks and feels for others as well as for himself. He sets the same value on other men's opinions as on his own. If he regards his on work as important, he sees also that the work of other men is equally important. He does not content for the merit of his own against the demerit of that of others. He is not overthrown, like Humptydumpty, with a sense of self importance. He has put aside egotism for truth, and he perceives the right relations of things. He has conquered irritability, and has come to see that there is nothing in itself that should cause irritation. As well be irritable with a pansy because it is not a rose, as a with a man because he does not see as you see. Minds differ, and the calm man recognizes the differences as facts in human nature.

The calm, impartial man, is not only the happiest man, he also has all his powers at his command. He is sure, deliberate, executive, and swiftly and easily accomplishes in silence what the irritable men slowly and laboriously toils through with much nice. His mind is purified, poised, concentrated, and is ready at any moment to be directed upon a given work with unerring power. In the calm mind all contradictions are reconciled, and there is radiant gladness and perpetual peace. As Emerson puts it: "Calmness is joy fixed and habitual."

One should not confound indifference with calmness, for it is at the opposite extreme. Indifference is lifelines, while calmness is glowing life and full orbed power. The calm man has partly or entirely conquered self, and having successfully battled with the selfishness within, he knows how to meet and overcome it successfully in others. In any moral content the calm man is always the victor. So long as he remains calm, defeat is impossible.

Self control is better than riches and calmness is a perpetual benediction.

Wisdom abides with the impartial man. Her counsels guide him; her wings shield him; she leads him along pleasant ways to happy destinations.

Wisdom is many sided. The wise man adapts himself to others. He acts for their good, yet never violates the moral virtues or the principles of right conduct. The foolish man cannot adapt himself to others; he acts for himself only, and continually violates the moral virtues and the principles of right conduct. There is a degree of wisdom in every act of impartiality, and once a man has touched and experience the impartial zone, he can recover it again and again until he finally establishes himself in it.

Every thought, word, and act of wisdom tells on the world at large, for it is fraught with greatness. Wisdom is a well of knowledge and a spring of power. It is profound and comprehensive, and is so exact and all inclusive as to embrace the smallest details. In its spacious greatness it does not overlook the small. The wise mind is like the world, it contains all things in their proper place and order, and is not burdened thereby. Like the world also, it is free, and unconscious of any restrictions; yet it is never loose, never erring, never inful and repentant. Wisdom is the steady, grown up being of whom folly was the crying infant. It was outgrown the weakness and dependence, the errors and punishments of infantile ignorance, and is erect, poised, strong, and serene.

The understanding mind needs no external support. It stands of itself on the firm ground of knowledge; not book-knowledge, but ripened experience. It has passed through all minds, and therefore knows them. It has traveled with all hearts, and knows their journeying in joy and sorrow.

When wisdom touches a man, he is lifted up and transfigured. He becomes a new being with new aims and powers, and he inhabits a new universe in which to accomplish a new and glorious destiny.

Such is the Pillar of impartiality which adds its massive strength and incomparable grace to support and beautify the Temple of Prosperity.

Eighth Pillar – Self-reliance

Every young man ought to read Emerson's essay on 'Self Reliance'. It is the manliest, most virile essay that was ever penned. It is calculated to cure alike those two mental maladies common to youth, namely, self depreciation and self conceit. It is almost as sure to reveal to the prig the smallness and emptiness of his vanity, as it is to show the bashful man the weakness and ineffectuality of his dividence. It is a new revelation of manly dignity; as much a revelation as any that was vouchsafed to ancient seer and prophet, and perhaps a more practical, eminently suited to his mechanic age, coming, as it does from a modern prophet of a new type and called in a new race, and its chief merit is its powerfully tonic quality.

Let not self-reliance be confounded with self conceit, for as high and excellent as is the one, just so low and worthless is other. There cannot be anything mean in self reliance, while in self conceit there cannot be anything great.

The man that never says "no" when questioned on subjects of which he is entirely ignorant, to avoid, as he imagines, being thought ignorant, but confidently puts forward guesses and assumptions as knowledge, will be known for his ignorance, and ill esteemed for his added conceit. An honest confession of ignorance will command respect where a conceited assumption of knowledge will elicit contempt.

The timid, apologetic man who seems almost afraid to live, who fears that he will do something not in the approved way, and will subject himself to ridicule, is not a full man. He must needs imitate others, and have no independent action. He needs that self reliance which will compel him to fall back on his own initiative, and so become a new example instead of the slavish follower of an old one. As for ridicule he who is hurt by it is no man. The shafts or mockery and sarcasm cannot pierce the strong armour of the self reliant man. They cannot reach the invincible citadel of his honest heart to sting or wound it. The sharp arrows of irony may rain upon him, but he laughs as they are deflected by the strong breast plate of his confidence, and fall harmless about him.

"Trust thyself," says Emerson, 'every heart vibrates to that iron string." Throughout the ages men have so far leaned, and do still lean, upon external makeshifts instead of standing upon their own native simplicity and original dignity. The few who have had the courage to so stand, have been singled out and elevated as heroes; and he is indeed the true hero who has the hardihood to let his nature speak for itself, who has that strong metal which enables him to stand upon his own intrinsic worth.

It is true that the candidate for such heroism must endure the test of strength. He must not be shamed from his ground by the bugbears of an initiate conventionalist. He must not fear for his reputation or position, or for his standing in the church or his prestige in local society. He must learn to act and live as independently of these consideration as he does of the current fashions in the antipodes. Yet when he has endured this test, and stander and odium have failed to move or afflict him, he has become a man indeed, one that society will have to reckon with, and finally accept on his own terms.

Sooner or later all men will turn or guidance to the self reliant man, and while the best minds do not make a prop of him, they respect and value his work and worth, and recognize his place among the goods that have gone before.

It must not be thought an indication of self reliance to scorn to learn. Such an attitude is born of a stubborn superciliousness which has the elements of weakness, and is prophetic of a fall, rather than the elements of strength and the promise of high achievement which are characteristic of self – reliance. Pride and vanity must not be associated with self rests upon incidentals and appurtenances – on money, clothing, property, prestige, position and these lost, all is lost. Self reliance rests upon essentials and principles on worth, probity, purity, sincerity, character, truth and whatever may be lost is of little account, for these are never lost. Pride tries to hide its ignorance by ostentation and assumption, and is unwilling to be thought a learner in any direction. It stands, during its little fleeting day, on ignorance and appear-ance, and the higher it is lifted up today the lower it will be cast down tomorrow. Self reliance has nothing to hide, and is willing to learn; and while there can be no humility where pride is, self reliance and humility are compatible, nay more, they are complementary, and the sublimes form of self reliance is only found associated with the profoundest humility. "Extremes meet" says Emerson "and there is no better example than the haughtiness of humility. No aristocrat, no prince born to the purple, can begin to compare with the self respect of the saint. Why is he so lowly, but that he knows that he can well afford it, resting on the largeness of God in him?" It was Buddha who, I this particular, said; — "Those who, either now or after I am dead, shall be a lamp unto themselves, relying upon them selves only and not relying upon any external help, but holding fast to the truth as their lamp, and seeking their salvation in the truth alone, shall not look for assistance to any one beside themselves, it is they, among my disciples, who shall reach the very top mist height. But they must be willing to learn." In this saying, the repeated insistence on the necessity for relying upon one's self alone, coupled with the final exhortation to be eager to learn, is the wisest utterance on self reliance that I know. In it, the Great Teacher comprehends that perfect balance between self trust and humility which the man of truth must acquire.

"Self – trust is the essence of heroism." All great men are self reliant, and we should use them as teachers and exemplars and not as props and perambulators. A great man comes who leans upon no one, but stands alone in the solitary dignity of truth, and straightway the world begins to lean upon him, begins to make him an excuse for spiritual indolence and a destructive self-abasement. Better than cradling our vices in the strength of the great would it be to newly light our virtues at their luminous lamp. If we rely upon the light of another, darkness will over take us, but if we rely upon our own light we have but to keep it burning. We may both draw light from another and communicate it, but to think it sufficient while our own lamp is rusting in neglect, is shortly to find ourselves abandoned in darkness. Our own inner light is the light which never fails us.

What is the "inner light" of the Quakers but another name for self reliance? We should stand upon what we are, not upon what another is. "But I am so small and poor," you say: well, stand upon that smallness, and presently it will become great. A babe must needs suckle and cling, but not so man. Henceforth he goes upon his own limbs. Men pray to God to put into their hands that which they are framed to reach out for; to put into their mouth the food for which they should strenuously labour. But men will outgrow this spiritual infancy. The time will come when men will no more pay a priest to pray for them and preach to them.

Man's chief trouble is a mistrust of himself, so that the self trusting man becomes a rare and singular spectacle. If a man look upon himself as a "worm," what can come out of him but an ineffectual wriggling. Truly, "He that humbleth shall be exalted," but not he that degardeth himself. A man should see himself as he is, and if there is any unworthiness in him, he should get rid of it, and retain and rely upon that which is of worth. A man is only debased when he debases himself; he is exalted when he lives an exalted life.

Why should a man, with ceaseless iterations, draw attention to his fallen nature? There is a false humility which takes a sort of pride in vice. If one has fallen, it is that he may rise and be the wiser for it. if a man falls into a ditch, he does not lie there and call upon every passer by to mark his fallen state, he gets up and goes on his way with greater care. So if one has fallen into the ditch of vice, let him rise and be cleansed, and go on his way rejoicing.

There is not a sphere in life wherein a man's influence and prosperity will not be considerably increased by even a measure of self reliance, and to the teacher – whether secular or religious to organizers, managers, overseers, and in all positions of control and command, it is an indispensable equipment.

The four grand qualities of self reliance are:—

1. Decision
2. Steadfastness
3. Dignity
4. Independence

Decision makes a man strong. The wearer is the weakling. A man who is to play a speaking part, however small, in the drama of life must be decisive and know what he is about. Whatever he doubts, he must not doubt his power to act. He must know his part in life, and put all his energy into it. He must have some solid ground of knowledge from which to work, and stand securely on that. It may be only the price and quality of stock, but he must know his work thoroughly, and know that he knows it. he must be ready at any time to answer for himself when his duty is impugned. He should be so well grounded upon his particular practice as not to be affected with hesitation on any point or in any emergence. It is a true saying that "the man that hesitates is lost." No one believes in him who does not believe in himself, who doubts, halts, and wavers, and cannot extricate himself from the tangled threads of two courses. Who would deal with a tradesman who did not know the price of his own goods, or was not sure where to find them? A man must know his business. If he does not know his own, who shall instruct him? He must be able to give a good report of the truth that is in him, must have that deceive touch which skill and knowledge only can impart.

Certainty is a great element in self reliance. To have weight, a man must have some truth to impart, and all skill is a communication of truth. He must "speak with authority, and not as the scribes." He must master something, and know that he has mastered it, so as to deal with it lucidly and under-standingly, in the way of a master, and not to remain always an apprentice.

Indecision is a disintegrating factor. A minute's faltering may turn back the current of success. Men who are afraid to decide quickly for fear of making a mistake, nearly always makes a mistake when they do act. The quickest, in thought and action, are less liable to blunder, and it is better to act with decision and make a mistake than to act with indecision and make a mistake than to act with indecision and make a mistake, for in the former case there is but error, but in the latter, weakness is added to error.

A man should be decided always, both where he knows and where he does not know. He should be as ready to say "no" as "yes," as quick to acknowledge his ignorance as to impart his knowledge. If he stands upon fact, and acts from the simple truth, he will find no room for halting between two opinions.

Make up your mind quickly, and act decisively. Better still, have a mind that is already made up and then decision will be instinctive and spontaneous.

Steadfastness arises in the mind that is quick to decide. It is indeed a final decision upon the best course of conduct and the best path in life. It is the vow of the soul to stand firmly by its principles whatever betide. It is neither necessary nor unnecessary that there by any written or spoken vow, for unswerving loyalty to a fixed principle is the spirit of all vows.

The man without fixed principles will not accomplish much. Expediency is a quagmire and a thorny waste, in which a man is continually sticking in the shifting mud of his own moral looseness, and is pricked and scratched with the thorns of his self created disappointments.

One must have some solid ground on which to stand among one's fellows. He cannot stand on the bog of concession. Shiftiness is a vice of weakness, and the vices of weakness do more to undermine character and influence than the vices of strength. The man that is vicious through excess of animal strength takes a shorter cut to truth – when his mind is made up that he who is vicious through lack of virility, and whose chief vice consists in not having a mind of his own upon anything. When one understands that power is adaptable to both good and bad ends, it will not surprise him that the drunkards and harlots should reach the kingdom of heaven before the diplomatic religionists. They are at least through in the course which they have adopted, vile though it be, and thoroughness is strength. It only needs that strength to be turned from bad to good, and lo! The loathed sinner has become the lofty saint!

A man should have a firm, fixed, determined mind. He should decide upon those principles which are best to stand by in all issues, and which will most safely guide him through the maze of conflicting opinions, and inspire him with unflinching courage in the battle of life. Having adopted his principles, they should be more to him than gain or happiness, more even than life itself, and if he never deserts them he will find that they will never desert him; they will defend him from all enemies, deliver him safely from all dangers, light up his pathway through all darkness and difficulties. They will be to him a light in darkness, a resting place from sorrow, and a refuge from the conflicts of the world.

Dignity clothes, as with a majestic garment, the steadfast mind. He who is as unyielding as a bar of steel when he is expected to compromise with evil, and as supple as a willow wand in adapting himself to that which is good, carries about with him a dignity that calms and uplifts others by its presence.

The unsteady mind, the mind that is not anchored to any fixed principles, that is stubborn where its own desires are threatened, and yielding where its own moral welfare is at stake, has no gravity, no balance, no calm composure.

The man of dignity cannot be down-trodden and enslaved, because he has ceased to tread upon and enslave himself. He at once disarms, with a look, a word, a wise and suggestive silence, any attempt to demean him. His mere presence is a wholesome reproof to the flippant and the unseemly, while it is a rock of strength to the lover of the good.

But the chief reason why the dignified man commands respect is, not only that he is supremely self respecting, but that he graciously treats all others with a due esteem. Pride loves itself, and treats those beneath it with supercilious contempt, for love of self and contempt for others are always found together in equal degrees, so that the greater the self love, the greater the arrogance. True dignity arises, not from self love, but from self sacrifice that is, from unbiased adherence to a fixed central principle. The dignity of the Judge arises from the fact that in the performance of his duty he sets aside all personal consideration, and stands solely upon the law; his little personality, impermanent and fleeting' becomes nothing, while the law, enduring and majestic, becomes all. Should a Judge, in deciding a case, forget the law, and fall into personal feeling and prejudice, his dignity would be gone. So with the man of stately purity of character, he stands upon the divine law, and not upon personal feeling, for immediately a man gives way to passion he has sacrificed dignity, and takes his place as one of the multitude of the unwise and uncontrolled.

Every man will have composure and dignity in the measure that he acts from a fixed principle. It only needs that the principle be right, and therefore unassailable. So long as man abides by such a principle, and does not waver or descend into the personal element, attacking passions, prejudices and interests, however powerful, will be weak and ineffectual before the unconquerable strength of an incorruptible principle, and will at last yield their combined and unseemly confusion to his single and majestic right.

Independence is the birthright of the strong and well controlled man. All men love and strive for liberty. All men aspire to some sort of freedom.

A man should labour for himself or for the community. Unless he is a cripple, a chronic invalid, or is mentally irresponsible, he should be ashamed to depend upon others for all he has, giving nothing in return. If one imagines that such a condition is freedom, let him know that it is one of the lowest forms of slavery. The time will come when, to be a drone in the human hive, even (as matters are now) a respectable drone and not a poor tramp, will be a public disgrace, and will be no longer respectable.

Independence, freedom, glorious liberty, come through labour and not from idleness, and the self reliant man is too strong, too honourable, too upright to depend upon others, like a sucking babe, for his support. He earns, with hand or brain, the right to live as becomes a man and a citizen; and this he does whether born rich or poor, for riches are no excuse for idleness; rather are they an opportunity to labour, with the rare facilities which they afford, for the good of the community.

Only he who is self supporting is free, self reliant, independent.

Thus is the nature of the Eight Pillars explained. On what foundation they rest, the manner of their building, their ingredients, the fourfold nature of the material of which each is composed, what positions they occupy, and how they support the Temple, all may now build; and he who knew but imperfectly may know more perfectly; and he who knew perfectly may rejoice in this systematization and simplification of the moral order in Prosperity. Let us now consider the Temple itself, that we may know the might of its Pillars, the strength of its walls, the endurance of its roof, and the architectural beauty and perfection of the whole.

The Temple of Prosperity

The reader who has followed the course of this book with a view to obtaining information on the details of money making, business transactions, profit and loss in various undertakings, prices, markets, agreements, contracts, and other matters connected with the achievement of prosperity, will have noted an entire absence of any instruction on these matters of detail. The reason for this is fourfold, namely:—

First. Details cannot stand alone, but are powerless to build up anything unless intelligently related to principles.

Second. Details are infinite, and are ceaselessly changing, while principles are few, and are eternal and unchangeable.

Third. Principles are the coherent factors in all details, regulating and harmonizing them, so that to have right principles is to be right in all the subsidiary details.

Fourth. A teacher of truth in any direction must adhere rigidly to principles, and must not allow himself to be drawn away from them into the ever-changing maze of private particulars and personal details, because such particulars and details have only a local right, and are only necessary for certain individuals, while principles are universally right and are necessary for all men.

He who grasps the principles of this book so as to be able to intelligently practice them, will be able to reach the heart of this fourfold reason. The details of a man's affairs are important, but they are his details or the details of his particular branch of industry, and all outside that branch are not concerned with them, but moral principles are the same for all men; they are applicable to all conditions, and govern all particulars.

The man who works from fixed principles does not need to harass himself over the complications of numerous details. He will grasp, as it were, the entire details in one single thought, and will see them through and through, illumined by the light of the principle to which they stand related, and this without friction, and with freedom from anxiety and strain.

Until principles are grasped, details are regarded, and dealt with, as primary matters, and so viewed they lead to innumerable complications and confused issues. In the light of principles, they are seen to be secondary facts, and so seen, all difficulties connected with them are at once overcome and annulled by a reference to principles.

He who is involved in numerous details without the regulating and synthesizing element of principles is like one lost in a forest, with no direct path along which to walk amid the mass of objects. He is swelled up by the details, while the man of principles contains all details within himself; he stands outside them, as it were, and grasps them in their entirety, while the other man can only see the few that are nearest to him at the time.

All things are contained in principles. They are the laws of things, and all things observe their own law. It is an error to view things apart from their nature. Details are the letter of which principles are the spirit. It is as true in art, science, literature, commerce, as in religion, that "the letter killeth, the spirit of giveth life." The body of a man, with its wonderful combination of parts, is important, but only in its relation to the spirit. The spirit being withdrawn, the body is useless and is put away. The body of a business, with all its complicated details is important, but only in its relation to the vivifying principles by which it is controlled. These withdrawn, the business will perish.

To have the body of prosperity – its material presentation – we must first have the spirit of prosperity, and the spirit of prosperity is the quick spirit of moral virtue. Moral blindness prevails. Men see money, property, pleasure, leisure, etc., and, mistaking them for prosperity, strive to get them for their own enjoyment, but, when obtained, they find no enjoyment in them.

Prosperity is at first a spirit, an attitude of mind, a moral power, a life, which manifests outwardly in the form of plenty, happiness, joy. Just as a man cannot become a genius by writing poems, essay as plays, but must develop and acquire the soul of genius – when the writing will follow as effect to cause — so one cannot become prosperous by hoarding up money, and by gaining property and possessions, but must develop and acquire the soul of virtue, when the material accessories will follow as effect to cause, for the spirit of virtue is the spirit of joy, and it contains within itself all abundance, all satisfaction, all fullness of life.

There is no joy in money, there is no joy in property, there is no joy in material accumulations or in any material things of itself. These things are dead and lifeless. The spirit of joy must be in the man or it is nowhere. He must have within him the capacity for happiness. He must have the wisdom to know how to use these things, and not merely hoard them. He must possess them, and not be possessed by them. They must be dependent upon him, and not he upon them. They must be dependent upon him, and not he upon them. They must follow him, and not be for ever be running after them; and they will inevitably follow him, if he has the moral elements within to which they are related.

Nothing is absent from the Kingdom of heaven; it contains all good, true, and necessary things, and "the Kingdom of God is within you." I know rich people who are supremely happy, because they are generous, magnanimous, pure and joyful; but I also know rich people who are very miserable, and these are they who looked to money and possessions for their happiness, and have not developed the spirit of good and of joy within themselves.

How can it be said of a wretched man that he is "prosperous," even if his income be ten thousand pounds a year? There must be fitness, and harmony, and satisfaction in a true prosperity. When a rich man is happy, it is that he brought the spirit of happiness to his riches, and not that the riches brought happiness to him. He is a full man with full material advantages and responsibilities, while the miserable rich man is an empty man looking to riches for that fullness of life which can only be evolved from within.

Thus prosperity resolves itself into a moral capacity, and in the wisdom to rightfully use and lawfully enjoy the material things which are inseparable from our earthly life. If one would be free without, let him first be free within, for if he be bound in a spirit by weakness, selfishness, or vice, how can the possession of money liberate him! Will it not rather become, in his hands, a ready instrument by which to further enslave himself?

The visible effects of prosperity, then, must not be considered alone, but in their relation to the mental and moral cause. There is a hidden foundation to every building; the fact that it continues to stands is proof of that. There is a hidden foundation to every from of established success; its permanence proves that it is so. Prosperity stands on the foundation of character, and there is not, in all the wide universe, any other foundation. True wealth is weal, welfare, well being, soundness, wholeness, and happiness. The wretched rich are not truly wealthy. They are merely encumbered with money, luxury, and leisure, as instruments of self torture. By their possessions they are self cursed.

The moral man is ever blessed, ever happy, and his life, viewed as a whole, is always a success. To these there is no exception, for whatever failures he may have in detail, the finished work of his life will be sound, whole, complete; and through all he will have a quiet conscience, an honorable name, and all manifold blessings which are inseparable from richness of character, and without this moral richness, financial riches will not avail or satisfy.

Let us briefly recapitulate, and again view the Eight Pillars in their strength and splendour.

Energy – Rousing one's self up to strenuous and unremitting exertion in the accomplishment of one's task.

Economy – Concentration of power, the conservation of both capital and character, the latter being mental capital, and therefore of the utmost importance.

Integrity – Unswerving honesty; keeping inviolate all promises, agreements, and contracts, apart from all considerations of loss or gain.

System – Making all details, subservient to order, and thereby relieving the memory and the mind of superfluous work and strain by reducing many to one.

Sympathy – Magnanimity, generosity, gentleness, and tenderness; being open handed, free, and kind.

Sincerity – Being sound and whole, robust and true; and therefore not being one person in public and another in private, and not assuming good actions openly while doing bad actions in secret.

Impartiality – Justice; not striving for self, but weighing both sides, and acting in accordance with equity.

Self – Reliance – Looking to one's self only for strength and support by standing on principles which are fixed and invincible, and not relying upon outward things which at any moment may be snatched away.

How can any life be other than successful which is built on these Eight Pillars? Their strength is such that no physical or intellectual strength can compare with it; and to have built all the eight perfectly would render a man invincible. It will be found, however, that men are often strong in one or several of these qualities, and weak in others, and it is this weak element that invites failure. It is foolish, for instance, to attribute a man's failure in business to his honest. It is impossible for honesty to produce failure. The cause of failure must be looked for in some other direction – in the lack, and not the possession, of some good necessary quality. Moreover, such attribution of failure to honesty is a slur on the integrity of commerce; and a false indict- ment of those men, numerous enough, who are honourably engaged in trade. A man may be strong in Energy, Economy, and System, but comparatively weak in the other five. Such a man will just fail of complete success by lacking one of the four corner pillars, namely, Integrity. His temple will give way at that weak corner, for the first four Pillars must be well built before the

Temple of Prosperity can stand secure. They are the first qualities to be acquired in a man's moral evolution, and without them the second four cannot be possessed. Again, if a man be strong in the first three, and lack the fourth, the absence of order will invite confusion and disaster into his affairs; and so on with any partial combination of these qualities, especially of the first four, for the second four are of so lofty a character that at present men can but possess them, with rare exceptions, in a more or less imperfect form. The man of the world, then, who wishes to secure an abiding success in any branch of commerce, or in one of the many lines of industry in which men are commonly engaged, must build into his character, by practice, the first four moral Pillars. By these fixed principles he must regulate his thought, his conduct, and his affairs; consulting them in every difficulty, making every detail serve them, and above all, never deserting them under any circumstance to gain some personal advantage or to save some personal trouble, for to so desert them is to make one's self vulnerable to the disintegrating elements of evil, and to become assailable to accusations from others. He who so abides by these four principles will achieve a full measure of success in his own particular work, whatever it may be; his Temple of Prosperity will be well built and well supported, and it will stand secure. The perfect practice of these four principles is within the scope of all men who are willing to study them with that object in view, for they are so simple and plain that a child could grasp their meaning, and their perfection in conduct does not call for an unusual degree of self sacrifice, though it demands some self denial and personal discipline without which there can be no success in this world of action. The second four pillars, however, are principles of a more profound nature, are more difficult to understand and practice, and call from the highest degree of self sacrifice and self effacement. Few, at present, can reach that detachment from the personal element which their perfect practice demands, but the few who accomplish this in any marked degree will vastly enlarge their powers and enrich their life, and will adorn their Temple of Prosperity with a singular and attractive beauty which will gladden and elevate all beholders long after they have passed away.

But those who are beginning to build their Temple of Prosperity in accordance with the teaching of this book, must bear in mind that a building requires time to erect, and it must be patiently raised up, brick upon brick and stone upon stone, and the Pillars must be firmly fixed and cemented, and labour and care will be needed to make the whole complete. And the building of this inner mental Temple is none the less real and substantial because invisible and noiseless, for in the raising up of his, as of Solomon's Temple which was "seven years in building" – it can be said, "there was neither hammer nor axe nor any tool of iron heard in the house, while it was in the building."

Even so, oh reader construct thy character, raise up the house of thy life, build up thy Temple of Prosperity. Be not as the foolish who rise and fall upon the uncertain flux of selfish desires: but be at peace in thy labour, crown thy career with completeness, and so be numbered among the wise who, without uncertainty, build upon a fixed and secure foundation – even upon the Principles of Truth which endure for ever.

Foundation Stones to Happiness and Success

Table of Contents

Editor's Preface

This is one of the last MSS. written by James Allen. Like all his works it is eminently practical. He never wrote theories, or for the sake of writing, or to add another to his many books; but he wrote when he had a message, and it became a message only when he had lived it out in his own life, and knew that it was good. Thus he wrote facts, which he had proven by practice.

To live out the teaching of this book faithfully in every detail of life will lead one to more than happiness and success — even to Blessedness, Satisfaction and Peace.

LILY L. ALLEN

Foreword

How does a man begin the building of a house? He first secures a plan of the proposed edifice, and then proceeds to build according to the plan, scrupulously following it in every detail, beginning with the foundation. Should he neglect the beginning — the beginning on a mathematical plan — his labour would be wasted, and his building, should it reach completion without tumbling to pieces, would be insecure and worthless. The same law holds good in any important work; the right beginning and first essential is a definite mental plan on which to build.

Nature will have no slipshod work, no slovenliness and she annihilates confusion, or rather, confusion is in itself annihilated. Order, definiteness, purpose, eternally prevail, and he who in his operations ignores these mathematical elements at once deprives himself of substantiality, complete-ness, happiness and success.

JAMES ALLEN

Right Principles

It is wise to know what comes first, and what to do first. To begin anything in the middle or at the end is to make a muddle of it. The athlete who began by breaking the tape would not receive the prize. He must begin by facing the starter and toeing the mark, and even then a good start is important if he is to win. The pupil does not begin with algebra and literature, but with counting and ABC. So in life – the businessmen who begin at the bottom achieve the more enduring success; and the religious men who reach the highest heights of spiritual knowledge and wisdom are they who have stooped to serve a patient apprenticeship to the humbler tasks, and have not scorned the common experiences of humanity, or overlooked the lessons to be learned from them.

The first things in a sound life — and therefore, in a truly happy and successful life — are right principles. Without right principles to begin with, there will be wrong practices to follow with, and a bungled and wretched life to end with. All the infinite variety of calculations which tabulate the commerce and science of the world, come out of the ten figures; all the hundreds of thousands of books which constitute the literature of the world, and perpetuate its thought and genius, are built up from the twenty-six letters. The greatest astronomer cannot ignore the ten simple figures. The profoundest man of genius cannot dispense with the twenty-six simple characters. The fundamentals in all things are few and simple: yet without them there is no knowledge and no achievement. The fundamentals — the basic principles — in life, or true living, are also few and simple, and to learn them thoroughly, and study how to apply them to all the details of life, is to avoid confusion, and to secure a substantial foundation for the orderly building up of an invincible character and a permanent success; and to succeed in comprehending those principles in their innumerable ramifications in the labyrinth of conduct, is to become a Master of Life.

The first principles in life are principles of conduct. To name them is easy. As mere words they are on all men's lips, but as fixed sources of action, admitting of no compromise, few have learned them. In this short talk I will deal with five only of these principles. These five are among the simplest of the root principles of life, but they are those that come nearest to the everyday life, for they touch the artisan the businessman, the householder, the citizen at every point. Not one of them can be dispensed with but at severe cost, and he who perfects himself in their application will rise superior to many of the troubles and failures of life, and will come into these springs and currents of thought which flow harmoniously towards the regions of enduring success. The first of these principles is —

DUTY — A much-hackneyed word, I know, but it contains a rare jewel for him who will seek it by assiduous application. The principle of duty means strict adherence to one's own business, and just as strict non-interference in the business of others. The man who is continually instructing others, gratis, how to manage their affairs, is the one who most mismanages his own. Duty also means undivided attention to the matter in hand, intelligent concentration of the mind on the work to be done; it includes all that is meant by thoroughness, exactness, and efficiency. The details of duties differ with individuals, and each man should know his own duty better then he knows his neighbour's, and better than his neighbour knows his; but although the working details differ, the principle is always the same. Who has mastered the demands of duty?

HONESTY is the next principle. It means not cheating or overcharging another. It involves the absence of all trickery, lying, and deception by word, look, or gesture. It includes sincerity, the saying what you mean, and the meaning what you say. It scorns cringing policy and shining compliment. It builds up good reputations, and good reputations build up good businesses, and bright joy accompanies well-earned success. Who has scaled the heights of Honesty?

ECONOMY is the third principle. The conservation of one's financial resources is merely the vestibule leading towards the more spacious chambers of true economy. It means, as well, the husbanding of one's physical vitality and mental resources. It demands the conservation of energy by the avoidance of enervating self-indulgences and sensual habits. It holds for its follower strength, endurance, vigilance, and capacity to achieve. It bestows great power on him who learns it well. Who has realized the supreme strength of Economy?

LIBERALITY follows economy. It is not opposed to it. Only the man of economy can afford to be generous. The spendthrift, whether in money, vitality, or mental energy, wasted so much on his own miserable pleasures as to have none left to bestow upon others. The giving of money is the smallest part of liberality. There is a giving of thoughts, and deeds, and sympathy, the bestowing of goodwill, the being generous towards calumniators and opponents. It is a principle that begets a noble, far-reaching influence. It brings loving friends and staunch comrades, and is the foe of loneliness and despair. Who has measured the breadth of Liberality?

SELF–CONTROL is the last of these five principles, yet the most important. Its neglect is the cause of vast misery, innumerable failures, and tens of thousands of financial, physical, and mental wrecks. Show me the businessman who loses his temper with a customer over some trivial matter, and I will show you a man who, by that condition of mind, is doomed to failure. If all men practised even the initial stages of self-control, anger, with its consuming and destroying fire, would be unknown. The lessons of patience, purity, gentleness, kindness, and steadfastness, which are contained in the principle of self-control, are slowly learned by men, yet until they are truly learned a man's character and success are uncertain and insecure. Where is the man who has perfected himself in Self-Control? Where he may be, he is a master indeed.

The five principles are five practices, five avenues to achievement, and five source of knowledge. It is an old saying and a good rule that "Practice makes perfect," and he who would make his own the wisdom which is inherent in those principles, must not merely have them on his lips, they must be established in his heart. To know them and receive what they alone can bring, he must do them, and give them out in his actions.

Sound Methods

From the five foregoing Right Principles, when they are truly apprehended and practised, will issue Sound Methods. Right principles are manifested in harmonious action, and method is to life what law is to the universe. Everywhere in the universe there is the harmonious adjustment of parts, and it is this symmetry and harmony that reveals a cosmos, as distinguished from chaos. So in human life, the difference between a true life and a false, between one purposeful and effective and one purposeless and weak, is one of method. The false life is an incoherent jumble of thoughts, passions, and actions; the true life is an orderly adjustment of all its parts. It is all the difference between a mass of lumber and a smoothly working efficient machine. A piece of machinery in perfect working order is not only a useful, but an admirable and attractive thing; but when its parts are all out of gear, and refuse to be readjusted, its usefulness and attractiveness are gone, and it is thrown on the scrap-heap. Likewise a life perfectly adjusted in all its parts so as to achieve the highest point of efficiency, is not only a powerful, but an excellent and beautiful thing; whereas a life confused, inconsistent, discordant, is a deplorable exhibition of wasted energy.

If life is to be truly lived, method must enter into, and regulate, every detail of it, as it enters and regulates every detail of the wondrous universe of which we form a part. One of the distinguishing differences between a wise man and a foolish is, that the wise man pays careful attention to the smallest things, while the foolish man slurs over them, or neglects them altogether. Wisdom consists in maintaining things on their right relations, in keeping all things, the smallest as well as the greatest, in their proper places and times. To violate order is to produce confusion and discord, and unhappiness is but another name for discord.

The good businessman knows that system is three parts of success, and that disorder means failure. The wise man knows that disciplined, methodical living is three parts of happiness, and that looseness means misery. What is a fool but one who thinks carelessly, acts rashly, and lives loosely? What is a wise man but one who thinks carefully, acts calmly, and lives consistently?

The true method does not end with the orderly arrangement of the material things and external relations of life; this is but its beginning; it enters into the adjustment of the mind — the discipline of the passions, the elimination and choice of words in speech, the logical arrangement of the thoughts, and the selection of right actions.

To achieve a life rendered sound, successful, and sweet by the pursuance of sound methods, one must begin, not by neglect of the little everyday things, but by assiduous attention to them. Thus the hour of rising is important, and its regularity significant; as also are the timing of retiring to rest, and the number of hours given to sleep. Between the regularity and irregularity of meals, and the care and carelessness with which they are eaten, is all the difference between a good and bad digestion (with all that this applies) and an irritable or comfortable frame of mind, with its train of good or bad consequences, for, attaching to these meal-times and meal-ways are matters of both physiological and psychological significance. The due division of hours for business and for play, not confusing the two, the orderly fitting in of all the details of one's business, times for solitude, for silent thought and for effective action, for eating and for abstinence — all these things must have their lawful place in the life of him whose "daily round" is to proceed with the minimum degree of friction, who is to get the most of usefulness, influence, and joy out of life.

But all this is but the beginning of that comprehensive method which embraces the whole life and being. When this smooth order and logical consistency is extended to the words and actions, to the thoughts and desires, then wisdom emerges from folly, and out of weakness comes power sublime. When a man so orders his mind as to produce a beautiful working harmony between all its parts, then he reaches the highest wisdom, the highest efficiency, the highest happiness.

But this is the end; and he who would reach the end must begin at the beginning. He must systematise and render logical and smooth the smallest details of his life, proceeding step by step towards the finished accomplishment. But each step will yield its own particular measure of strength and gladness.

To sum up, method produces that smoothness which goes with strength and efficiency. Discipline is method applied to the mind. It produces that calmness which goes with power and happiness. Method is working by rule; discipline is living by rule. But working and living are not separate; they are but two aspects of character, of life.

Therefore, be orderly in work; be accurate in speech, be logical in thought. Between these and slovenliness, inaccuracy and confusion, is the difference between success and failure, music and discord, happiness and misery.

The adoption of sound methods of working, acting, thinking – in a word, of living, is the surest and safest foundation for sound health, sound success, sound peace of mind. The foundation of unsound methods will be found to be unstable, and to yield fear and unrest even while it appears to succeed, and when its time of failure comes, it is grievous indeed.

True Actions

Following on Right Principles and Methods come True Actions. One who is striving to grasp true principles and work with sound methods will soon come to perceive that details of conduct cannot be overlooked — that, indeed, those details are fundamentally distinctive or creative, according to their nature, and are, therefore, of deep significance and comprehensive importance; and this perception and knowledge of the nature and power of passing actions will gradually open and grow within him as an added vision, a new revelation. As he acquires this insight his progress will be more rapid, his pathway in life more sure, his days more serene and peaceful; in all things he will go the true and direct way, unswayed and untroubled by the external forces that play around and about him. Not that he will be indifferent to the welfare and happiness of those about him; that is quite another thing; but he will be indifferent to their opinions, to their ignorance, to their ungoverned passions. By True Actions, indeed, is meant acting rightly towards others, and the right-doer knows that actions in accordance with truth are but for the happiness of those about him, and he will do them even though an occasion may arise when some one near to him may advise or implore him to do otherwise.

True actions may easily be distinguished from false by all who wish so to distinguish in order that they may avoid false action, and adopt true. As in the material world we distinguish things by their form, colour, size, etc., choosing those things which we require, and putting by those things which are not useful to us, so in the spiritual world of deeds, we can distinguish between those that are bad and those that are good by their nature, their aim, and their effect and can choose and adopt those that are good, and ignore those that are bad.

In all forms of progress, avoidance of the bad always precedes acceptance and knowledge of the good, just as a child at school learns to do its lessons right by having repeatedly pointed out to it how it has done them wrong. If one does not know what is wrong and how to avoid it, how can he know what is right and how to practise it? Bad, or untrue, actions are those that spring from a consideration of one's own happiness only, and ignore the happiness of others, that arise in violent disturbances of the mind and unlawful desires, or that call for concealment in order to avoid undesirable complications. Good or true actions are those that spring from a consideration for others, that arise in calm reason and harmonious thought framed on moral principles or that will not involve the doer in shameful consequences if brought into the full light of day.

The right-doer will avoid those acts of personal pleasure and gratification which by their nature bring annoyance, pain, or suffering to others, no matter how insignificant those actions may appear to be. He will begin by putting away these; he will gain a knowledge of the unselfish and true by first sacrificing the selfish and untrue. He will learn not to speak or act in anger, or envy, or resentment, but will study how to control his mind, and will restore it to calmness before acting; and, most important of all, he will avoid, as he would the drinking of deadly poison, those acts of trickery, deceit, double-dealing, in order to gain some personal profit of advantage, and which lead, sooner or later, to exposure and shame for the doer of them. If a man is prompted to do a thing which he needs to conceal, and which he would not lawfully and frankly defend if it were examined of witness, he should know by that that it is a wrong act and therefore to be abandoned without a further moment's consideration.

The carrying out of this principle of honesty and sincerity of action, too, will further lead him into such a path of thoughtfulness in right-doing as will enable him to avoid doing those things which would involve him in the deceptive practices of other people. Before signing papers, or entering into verbal or written arrangements, or engaging himself to others in any way at their request, particularly if they be strangers, he will first inquire into the nature of the work or undertaking, and so, enlightened, he will know exactly what to do, and will be fully aware of the import of his action. To the right-doer thoughtlessness is a crime. Thousands of actions done with good intent lead to disastrous consequences because they are acts of thoughtlessness, and it is well said "that the way to hell is paved with good intentions." The man of true actions is, above all things, thoughtful:— "Be ye therefore wise as serpents and harmless as doves."

The term Thoughtlessness covers a wide field in the realm of deeds. It is only by increasing in thoughtfulness that a man can come to understand the nature of actions, and can, thereby, acquire the power of always doing that which is right. It is impossible for a man to be thoughtful and act foolishly. Thoughtfulness embraces wisdom.

It is not enough that an action is prompted by a good impulse or intention; it must arise in thoughtful consideration if it is to be a true action; and the man who wishes to be permanently happy in himself and a power for good to others must concern himself only with true actions. "I did it with the best of intentions," is a poor excuse from one who has thoughtlessly involved himself in the wrong-doing of others. His bitter experience should teach him to act more thoughtfully in the future.

True actions can only spring from a true mind, and therefore while a man is learning to distinguish and choose between the false and the true, he is correcting and perfecting his mind, and is thereby rendering it more harmonious and felicitous, more efficient and powerful. As he acquires the "inner eye" to clearly distinguish the right in all the details of life, and the faith and knowledge to do it, he will realise that he is building the house of his character and life upon a rock which the winds of failure and the storms of persecution can never undermine.

True Speech

Truth is known by practice only. Without sincerity there can be no knowledge of Truth; and true speech is the beginning of all sincerity. Truth in all its native beauty and original simplicity consists in abandoning and not doing all those things which are untrue, and in embracing and doing all those things which are true. True speech is therefore one of the elementary beginnings in the life of Truth. Falsehood, and all forms of deception; slander and all forms of evil-speaking — these must be totally abandoned and abolished before the mind can receive even a small degree of spiritual enlightenment. The liar and slanderer is lost in darkness; so deep is his darkness that he cannot distinguish between good and evil, and he persuades himself that his lying and evil-speaking are necessary and good, that he is thereby protecting himself and other people.

Let the would-be student of "higher things" look to himself and beware of self-delusion. If he is given to uttering words that deceive, or to speaking evil of others – if he speaks in insincerity, envy, or malice — then he has not yet begun to study higher things. He may be studying metaphysics, or miracles, or psychic phenomena, or astral wonders – he may be studying how to commune with invisible beings, to travel invisibly during sleep, or to produce curious phenomena — he may even study spirituality theoretically and as a mere book study, but if he is a deceiver and a backbiter, the higher life is hidden from him. For the higher things are these – uprightness, sincerity, innocence, purity, kindness, gentleness, faithfulness, humility, patience, pity, sympathy, self-sacrifice, joy, goodwill, love – and he who would study them, know them, and make them his own, must practice them, there is no other way.

Lying and evil-speaking belong to the lowest forms of spiritual ignorance, and there can be no such thing as spiritual enlightenment while they are practised. Their parents are selfishness and hatred.

Slander is akin to lying, but it is even more subtle, as it is frequently associated with indignation, and by assuming more successfully the appearance of truth, it ensnares many who would not tell a deliberate falsehood. For there are two sides to slander — there is the making of repeating of it, and there is the listening to it and acting upon it. The slanderer would be powerless without a listener. Evil words require an ear that is receptive to evil in which they may fall, before they can flourish; therefore he who listens to a slanderer, who believes it, and allows himself to be influenced against the person whose character and reputation are defamed, is in the same position as the one who framed or repeated the evil report. The evil-speaker is a positive slanderer; the evil-listener is a passive slanderer. The two are co-operators in the propagation of evil.

Slander is a common vice and a dark and deadly one. An evil report begins in ignorance, and pursues its blind way in darkness. It generally takes its rise in a misunderstanding. Some one feels that he or she has been badly treated, and, filled with indignation and resentment, unburdens himself to his friends and others in vehement language, exaggerating the enormity of the supposed offence on account of the feeling of injury by which he is possessed; he is listened to and sympathised with; the listeners, without hearing the other person's version of what has taken place, and on no other proof than the violent words of an angry man or woman, become cold in their attitude towards the one spoken against, and repeat to others what they have been told, and as such repetition is always more or less inaccurate, a distorted and altogether untrue report is soon passing from mouth to mouth.

It is because slander is such a common vice that it can work the suffering and injury that it does. It is because so many (not deliberate wrong-doers, and unconscious of the nature of the evil into which they so easily fall) are ready to allow themselves to be influenced against one whom they have hitherto regarded as honourable, that an evil report can do its deadly work. Yet its work is only amongst those who have not altogether acquired the virtue of true speech, the cause of which is a truth-loving mind. When one who has not entirely freed himself from repeating or believing an evil report about another, hears of an evil report about himself, his mind becomes aflame with burning resentment, his sleep is broken and his peace of mind is destroyed. He thinks the cause of all his suffering is in the other man and what that man has said about him, and is ignorant of the truth that the root and cause of his suffering lies in his own readiness to believe an evil report about another. The virtuous man — he who has attained to true speech, and whose mind is sealed against even the appearance of evil-speaking — cannot be injured and disturbed about any evil reports concerning himself; and although his reputation may for a time be stained in the minds of those who are prone to suggestions of evil, his integrity remains untouched and his character unsoiled; for no one can be stained by the evil deeds of another, but only by his own wrongdoing. And so, through all misrepresentation, misunderstanding, and contumely, he is untroubled and unrevengeful; his sleep is undisturbed, and his mind remains in peace.

True speech is the beginning of a pure, wise and well-ordered life. If one would attain to purity of life, if he would lessen the evil and suffering of the world, let him abandon falsehood and slander in thought and word, let him avoid even the appearance of these things, for there are no lies and slanders so deadly as those which are half-truths, and let him not be a participant in evil-speaking by listening to it. Let him also have compassion on the evil-speaker, knowing how such a one is binding himself to suffering and unrest; for no liar can know the bliss of Truth; no slanderer can enter the kingdom of peace.

By the words which he utters is a man's spiritual condition declared; by these also is he finally and infallibly adjudged, for as the Divine Master of the Christian world has declared, "By thy words shalt thou be justified, and by thy words shalt thou be condemned.

Equal-Mindedness

To be equally-minded is to be peacefully-minded, for a man cannot be said to have arrived at peace who allows his mind to be disturbed and thrown off the balance by occurrences.

The man of wisdom is dispassionate, and meets all things with the calmness of a mind in repose and free from prejudice. He is not a partisan, having put away passion, and he is always at peace with himself and the world, not taking sides nor defending himself, but sympathising with all.

The partisan is so convinced that his own opinion and his own side is right, and all that goes contrary to them is wrong, that he cannot think there is any good in the other opinion and the other side. He lives in a continual fever of attack and defence, and has no knowledge of the quiet peace of an equal mind.

The equal-minded man watches himself in order to check and overcome even the appearance of passion and prejudice in his mind, and by so doing he develops sympathy for others, and comes to understand their position and particular state of mind; and as he comes to understand others, he perceives the folly of condemning them and opposing himself to them. Thus there grows up in his heart a divine charity which cannot be limited, but which is extended to all things that live and strive and suffer.

When a man is under the sway of passion and prejudice he is spiritually blind. Seeing nothing but good in his own side, and nothing but evil in the other, he cannot see anything as it really is, not even his own side; and not understanding himself, he cannot understand the hearts of others, and thinks it is right that he should condemn them. Thus there grows up in his heart a dark hatred for those who refuse to see with him and who condemn him in return, he becomes separated from his fellow-men, and confines himself to a narrow torture chamber of his own making.

Sweet and peaceful are the days of the equal-minded man, fruitful in good, and rich in manifold blessings. Guided by wisdom, he avoids those pathways which lead down to hatred and sorrow and pain, and takes those which lead up to love and peace and bliss. The occurrences of life do not trouble him, nor does he grieve over those things which are regarded by mankind as grievous, but which must befall all men in the ordinary course of nature. He is neither elated by success nor cast down by failure. He sees the events of his life arrayed in their proper proportions, and can find no room for selfish wishes or vain regrets, for vain anticipations and childish disappointments.

And how is this equal-mindedness — this blessed state of mind and life — acquired? Only by overcoming one's self, only by purifying one's own heart, for the purification of the heart leads to unbiased comprehension, unbiased comprehension leads to equal-mindedness, and equal-mindedness leads to peace. The impure man is swept helplessly away on the waves of passion; the pure man guides himself into the harbour of rest. The fool says, "I have an opinion;" the wise man goes about his business.

Good Results

A considerable portion of the happenings of life comes to us without any direct choosing on our part, and such happenings are generally regarded as having no relation to our will or character, but as appearing fortuitously; as occurring without a cause. Thus one is spoken of as being "lucky," and another "unlucky," the inference being that each has received something which he never earned, never caused. Deeper thought, and a clearer insight into life convinces us, however, that nothing happens without a cause, and that cause and effect are always related in perfect adjustment and harmony. This being so, every happening directly affecting us is intimately related to our own will and character, is, indeed, an effect justly related to a cause having its seat in our consciousness. In a word, involuntary happenings of life are the results of our own thoughts and deeds. This, I admit, is not apparent on the surface; but what fundamental law, even in the physical universe, is so apparent? If thought, investigation, and experiment are necessary to the discovery of the principles which relate one material atom to another, even so are they imperative to the perception and understanding of the mode of action which relate one mental condition to another; and such modes, such laws, are known by the right-doer, by him who has acquired an understanding mind by the practice of true actions.

We reap as we sow. Those things which come to us, though not by our own choosing, are by our causing. The drunkard did not choose the delirium tremens or insanity which overtook him, but he caused it by his own deeds. In this case the law is plain to all minds, but where it is not so plain, it is nonetheless true. Within ourselves is the deep-seated cause of all our sufferings, the spring of all our joys. Alter the inner world of thoughts, and the other world of events will cease to bring you sorrow; make the heart pure, and to you all things will be pure, all occurrences happy and in true order.

"Within yourselves deliverance must be sought,
Each man his prison makes.
Each hath such lordship as the loftiest ones;

Nay, for with Powers above, around, below,
As with all flesh and whatsoever lives,
Act maketh joy or woe."

Our life is good or bad, enslaved or free, according to its causation in our thoughts, for out of these thoughts spring all our deeds, and from these deeds come equitable results. We cannot seize good results violently, like a thief, and claim and enjoy them, but we can bring them to pass by setting in motion the causes within ourselves.

Men strive for money, sigh for happiness, and would gladly possess wisdom, yet fail to secure these things, while they see others to whom these blessings appear to come unbidden. The reason is that they have generated causes which prevent the fulfilment of their wishes and efforts.

Each life is a perfectly woven network of causes and effects, of efforts (or lack of efforts) and results, and good results can only be reached by initiating good efforts, good causes. The doer of true actions, who pursues sound methods, grounded on right principles will not need to strive and struggle for good results; they will be there as the effects of his righteous rule of life. He will reap the fruit of his own actions and the reaping will be in gladness and peace.

This truth of sowing and reaping in the moral sphere is a simple one, yet men are slow to understand and accept it. We have been told by a Wise One that "the children of darkness are wiser in their day than the children of light", and who would expect, in the material world, to reap and eat where he had not sown and planted? Or who would expect to reap wheat in the field where he had sown tares, and would fall to weeping and complaining if he did not? Yet this is just what men do in the spiritual field of mind and deed. They do evil, and expect to get from it good, and when the bitter harvesting comes in all its ripened fullness, they fall into despair, and bemoan the hardness and injustice of their lot, usually attributing it to the evil deeds of others, refusing even to admit the possibility of its cause being hidden in themselves, in their own thoughts and deeds. The children of light — those who are searching for the fundamental principles of right living, with a view to making themselves into wise and happy beings – must train themselves to observe this law of cause and effect in thought, word and deed, as implicitly and obediently as the gardener obeys the law of sowing and reaping. He does not even question the law; he recognises and obeys it. When the wisdom which he instinctively practices in his garden, is practiced by men in the garden of their minds – when the law of the sowing of deeds is so fully recognised that it can no longer be doubted or questioned – then it will be just as faithfully followed by the sowing of those actions which will bring about a reaping of happiness and well-being for all. As the children of matter obey the laws of matter, so let the children of spirit obey the laws of spirit, for the law of matter and the law of spirit are one; they are but two aspects of one thing; the out-working of one principle in opposite directions.

If we observe right principles, or causes, wrong effects cannot possibly accrue. If we pursue sound methods, no shoddy thread can find its way into the web of our life, no rotten brick enter into the building of our character to render it insecure; and if we do true actions, what but good results can come to pass; for to say that good causes can produce bad effects is to say that nettles can be reaped from a sowing of corn.

He who orders his life along the moral lines thus briefly enunciated, will attain to such a state of insight and equilibrium as to render him permanently happy and perennially glad; all his efforts will be seasonally planted; all the issues of his life will be good, and though he may not become a millionaire as indeed he will have no desire to become such – he will acquire the gift of peace, and true success will wait upon him as its commanding master.

The Path to Prosperity

Table of Contents

Foreword

I looked around upon the world, and saw that it was shadowed by sorrow and scorched by the fierce fires of suffering. And I looked for the cause. I looked around, but could not find it; I looked in books, but could not find it; I looked within, and found there both the cause and the self-made nature of that cause. I looked again, and deeper, and found the remedy.

I found one Law, the Law of Love; one Life, the Life of adjustment to that Law; one Truth, the truth of a conquered mind and a quiet and obedient heart. And I dreamed of writing a book which should help men and women, whether rich or poor, learned or unlearned, worldly or unworldly, to find within themselves the source of all success, all happiness, all accomplishment, all truth. And the dream remained with me, and at last became substantial; and now I send it forth into the world on its mission of healing and blessedness, knowing that it cannot fail to reach the homes and hearts of those who are waiting and ready to receive it.

James Allen

The Lesson of Evil

Unrest and pain and sorrow are the shadows of life. There is no heart in all the world that has not felt the sting of pain, no mind has not been tossed upon the dark waters of trouble, no eye that has not wept the hot blinding tears of unspeakable anguish.

There is no household where the Great Destroyers, disease and death, have not entered, severing heart from heart, and casting over all the dark pall of sorrow. In the strong, and apparently indestructible meshes of evil all are more or less fast caught, and pain, unhappiness, and misfortune wait upon mankind.

With the object of escaping, or in some way mitigating this overshadowing gloom, men and women rush blindly into innumerable devices, pathways by which they fondly hope to enter into a happiness which will not pass away.

Such are the drunkard and the harlot, who revel in sensual excitements; such is the exclusive aesthete, who shuts himself out from the sorrows of the world, and surrounds himself with enervating luxuries; such is he who thirsts for wealth or fame, and subordinates all things to the achievement of that object; and such are they who seek consolation in the performance of religious rites.

And to all the happiness sought seems to come, and the soul, for a time, is lulled into a sweet security, and an intoxicating forgetfulness of the existence of evil; but the day of disease comes at last, or some great sorrow, temptation, or misfortune breaks suddenly in on the unfortified soul, and the fabric of its fancied happiness is torn to shreds.

So over the head of every personal joy hangs the Damocletian sword of pain, ready, at any moment, to fall and crush the soul of him who is unprotected by knowledge.

The child cries to be a man or woman; the man and woman sigh for the lost felicity of childhood. The poor man chafes under the chains of poverty by which he is bound, and the rich man often lives in fear of poverty, or scours the world in search of an elusive shadow he calls happiness.

Sometimes the soul feels that it has found a secure peace and happiness in adopting a certain religion, in embracing an intellectual philosophy, or in building up an intellectual or artistic ideal; but some overpowering temptation proves the religion to be inadequate or insufficient; the theoretical philosophy is found to be a useless prop; or in a moment, the idealistic statue upon which the devotee has for years been laboring, is shattered into fragments at his feet.

Is there, then, no way of escape from pain and sorrow? Are there no means by which bonds of evil may be broken? Is permanent happiness, secure prosperity, and abiding peace a foolish dream?

No, there is a way, and I speak it with gladness, by which evil can be slain for ever; there is a process by which disease, poverty, or any adverse condition or circumstance can be put on one side never to return; there is a method by which a permanent prosperity can be secured, free from all fear of the return of adversity, and there is a practice by which unbroken and unending peace and bliss can be partaken of and realized.

And the beginning of the way which leads to this glorious realization is the acquirement of a right understanding of the nature of evil.

It is not sufficient to deny or ignore evil; it must be understood. It is not enough to pray to God to remove the evil; you must find out why it is there, and what lesson it has for you.

It is of no avail to fret and fume and chafe at the chains which bind you; you must know why and how you are bound. Therefore, reader, you must get outside yourself, and must begin to examine and understand yourself.

You must cease to be a disobedient child in the school of experience and must begin to learn, with humility and patience, the lessons that are set for your edification and ultimate perfection; for evil, when rightly understood, is found to be, not an unlimited power or principle in the universe, but a passing phase of human experience, and it therefore becomes a teacher to those who are willing to learn.

Evil is not an abstract some thing outside yourself; it is an experience in your own heart, and by patiently examining and rectifying your heart you will be gradually led into the discovery of the origin and nature of evil, which will necessarily be followed by its complete eradication.

All evil is corrective and remedial, and is therefore not permanent. It is rooted in ignorance, ignorance of the true nature and relation of things, and so long as we remain in that state of ignorance, we remain subject to evil.

There is no evil in the universe which is not the result of ignorance, and which would not, if we were ready and willing to learn its lesson, lead us to higher wisdom, and then vanish away. But men remain in evil, and it does not pass away because men are not willing or prepared to learn the lesson which it came to teach them.

I knew a child who, every night when its mother took it to bed, cried to be allowed to play with the candle; and one night, when the mother was off guard for a moment, the child took hold of the candle; the inevitable result followed, and the child never wished to play with the candle again.

By its one foolish act it learned, and learned perfectly the lesson of obedience, and entered into the knowledge that fire burns. And, this incident is a complete illustration of the nature, meaning, and ultimate result of all sin and evil.

As the child suffered through its own ignorance of the real nature of fire, so older children suffer through their ignorance of the real nature of the things which they weep for and strive after, and which harm them when they are secured; the only difference being that in the latter case the ignorance and evil are more deeply rooted and obscure.

Evil has always been symbolized by darkness, and Good by light, and hidden within the symbol is contained the perfect interpretation, the reality; for, just as light always floods the universe, and darkness is only a mere speck or shadow cast by a small body intercepting a few rays of the illimitable light, so the Light of the Supreme Good is the positive and life-giving power which floods the universe, and evil the insignificant shadow cast by the self that intercepts and shuts off the illuminating rays which strive for entrance.

When night folds the world in its black impenetrable mantle, no matter how dense the darkness, it covers but the small space of half our little planet, while the whole universe is ablaze with living light, and every soul knows that it will awake in the light in the morning.

Know, then, that when the dark night of sorrow, pain, or misfortune settles down upon your soul, and you stumble along with weary and uncertain steps, that you are merely intercepting your own personal desires between yourself and the boundless light of joy and bliss, and the dark shadow that covers you is cast by none and nothing but yourself.

And just as the darkness without is but a negative shadow, an unreality which comes from nowhere, goes to nowhere, and has no abiding dwelling place, so the darkness within is equally a negative shadow passing over the evolving and Lightborn soul.

"But," I fancy I hear someone say, "why pass through the darkness of evil at all?" Because, by ignorance, you have chosen to do so, and because, by doing so, you may understand both good and evil, and may the more appreciate the light by having passed through the darkness.

As evil is the direct outcome of ignorance, so, when the lessons of evil are fully learned, ignorance passes away, and wisdom takes its place. But as a disobedient child refuses to learn its lessons at school, so it is possible to refuse to learn the lessons of experience, and thus to remain in continual darkness, and to suffer continually recurring punishments in the form of disease, disappointment, and sorrow.

He, therefore, who would shake himself free of the evil which encompasses him, must be willing and ready to learn, and must be prepared to undergo that disciplinary process without which no grain of wisdom or abiding happiness and peace can be secured.

A man may shut himself up in a dark room, and deny that the light exists, but it is everywhere without, and darkness exists only in his own little room.

So you may shut out the light of Truth, or you may begin to pull down the walls of prejudice, self-seeking and error which you have built around yourself, and so let in the glorious and omnipresent Light.

By earnest self-examination strive to realize, and not merely hold as a theory, that evil is a passing phase, a self-created shadow; that all your pains, sorrows and misfortunes have come to you by a process of undeviating and absolutely perfect law; have come to you because you deserve and require them, and that by first enduring, and then understanding them, you may be made stronger, wiser, nobler.

When you have fully entered into this realization, you will be in a position to mould your own circumstances, to transmute all evil into good and to weave, with a master hand, the fabric of your destiny.

What of the night, O Watchman! see'st thou yet
The glimmering dawn upon the mountain heights,
The golden Herald of the Light of lights,
Are his fair feet upon the hilltops set?

Cometh he yet to chase away the gloom,
And with it all the demons of the Night?
Strike yet his darting rays upon thy sight?
Hear'st thou his voice, the sound of error's doom?

The Morning cometh, lover of the Light;
Even now He gilds with gold the mountain's brow,
Dimly I see the path whereon even now
His shining feet are set toward the Night.

Darkness shall pass away, and all the things
That love the darkness, and that hate the Light
Shall disappear for ever with the Night:
Rejoice! for thus the speeding Herald sings.

The World a Reflex of Mental States

What you are, so is your world. Everything in the universe is resolved into your own inward experience. It matters little what is without, for it is all a reflection of your own state of consciousness.

It matters everything what you are within, for everything without will be mirrored and colored accordingly.

All that you positively know is contained in your own experience; all that you ever will know must pass through the gateway of experience, and so become part of yourself.

Your own thoughts, desires, and aspirations comprise your world, and, to you, all that there is in the universe of beauty and joy and bliss, or of ugliness and sorrow and pain, is contained within yourself.

By your own thoughts you make or mar your life, your world, your universe, As you build within by the power of thought, so will your outward life and circumstances shape themselves accordingly.

Whatsoever you harbor in the inmost chambers of your heart will, sooner or later by the inevitable law of reaction, shape itself in your outward life.

The soul that is impure, sordid and selfish, is gravitating with unerring precision toward misfortune and catastrophe; the soul that is pure, unselfish, and noble is gravitating with equal precision toward happiness and prosperity.

Every soul attracts its own, and nothing can possibly come to it that does not belong to it. To realize this is to recognize the universality of Divine Law.

The incidents of every human life, which both make and mar, are drawn to it by the quality and power of its own inner thought-life. Every soul is a complex combination of gathered experiences and thoughts, and the body is but an improvised vehicle for its manifestation.

What, therefore, your thoughts are, that is your real self; and the world around, both animate and inanimate, wears the aspect with which your thoughts clothe it.

"All that we are is the result of what we have thought. It is founded on our thoughts; it is made up of our thoughts." Thus said Buddha, and it therefore follows that if a man is happy, it is because he dwells in happy thoughts; if miserable, because he dwells in despondent and debilitating thoughts,

Whether one be fearful or fearless, foolish or wise, troubled or serene, within that soul lies the cause of its own state or states, and never without. And now I seem to hear a chorus of voices exclaim, "But do you really mean to say that outward circumstances do not affect our minds?" I do not say that, but I say this, and know it to be an infallible truth, that circumstances can only affect you in so far as you allow them to do so.

You are swayed by circumstances because you have not a right understanding of the nature, use, and power of thought.

You believe (and upon this little word belief hang all our sorrows and joys) that outward things have the power to make or mar your life; by so doing you submit to those outward things, confess that you are their slave, and they your unconditional master; by so doing, you invest them with a power which they do not, of themselves, possess, and you succumb, in reality, not to the mere circumstances, but to the gloom or gladness, the fear or hope, the strength or weakness, which your thought-sphere has thrown around them.

I knew two men who, at an early age, lost the hard-earned savings of years. One was very deeply troubled, and gave way to chagrin, worry, and despondency.

The other, on reading in his morning paper that the bank in which his money was deposited had hopelessly failed, and that he had lost all, quietly and firmly remarked, "Well, it's gone, and trouble and worry won't bring it back, but hard work will."

He went to work with renewed vigor, and rapidly became prosperous, while the former man, continuing to mourn the loss of his money, and to grumble at his "bad luck," remained the sport and tool of adverse circumstances, in reality of his own weak and slavish thoughts.

The loss of money was a curse to the one because he clothed the event with dark and dreary thoughts; it was a blessing to the other, because he threw around it thoughts of strength, of hope, and renewed endeavor.

If circumstances had the power to bless or harm, they would bless and harm all men alike, but the fact that the same circumstances will be alike good and bad to different souls proves that the good or bad is not in the circumstance, but only in the mind of him that encounters it.

When you begin to realize this you will begin to control your thoughts, to regulate and discipline your mind, and to rebuild the inward temple of your soul, eliminating all useless and superfluous material, and incorporating into your being thoughts alone of joy and serenity, of strength and life, of compassion and love, of beauty and immortality; and as you do this you will become joyful and serene, strong and healthy, compassionate and loving, and beautiful with the beauty of immortality.

And as we clothe events with the drapery of our own thoughts, so likewise do we clothe the objects of the visible world around us, and where one sees harmony and beauty, another sees revolting ugliness.

An enthusiastic naturalist was one day roaming the country lanes in pursuit of his hobby, and during his rambles came upon a pool of brackish water near a farmyard.

As he proceeded to fill a small bottle with the water for the purpose of examination under the microscope, he dilated, with more enthusiasm than discretion, to an uncultivated son of the plough who stood close by, upon the hidden and innumerable wonders contained in the pool, and concluded by saying, "Yes, my friend, within this pool is contained a hundred, nay, a million universes, had we but the sense or the instrument by which we could apprehend them." And the unsophisticated one ponderously remarked, "I know the water be full o' tadpoles, but they be easy to catch."

Where the naturalist, his mind stored with the knowledge of natural facts, saw beauty, harmony, and hidden glory, the mind unenlightened upon those things saw only an offensive mud-puddle.

The wild flower which the casual wayfarer thoughtlessly tramples upon is, to the spiritual eye of the poet, an angelic messenger from the invisible.

To the many, the ocean is but a dreary expanse of water on which ships sail and are sometimes wrecked; to the soul of the musician it is a living thing, and he hears, in all its changing moods, divine harmonies.

Where the ordinary mind sees disaster and confusion, the mind of the philosopher sees the most perfect sequence of cause and effect, and where the materialist sees nothing but endless death, the mystic sees pulsating and eternal life.

And as we clothe both events and objects with our own thoughts, so likewise do we clothe the souls of others in the garments of our thoughts.

The suspicious believe everybody to be suspicious; the Liar feels secure in the thought that he is not so foolish as to believe that there is such a phenomenon as a strictly truthful person; the envious see envy in every soul; the miser thinks everybody is eager to get his money; he who has subordinated conscience in the making of his wealth, sleeps with a revolver under his pillow, wrapped in the delusion that the world is full of conscienceless people who are eager to rob him, and the abandoned sensualist looks upon the saint as a hypocrite.

On the other hand, those who dwell in loving thoughts, see that in all which calls forth their love and sympathy; the trusting and honest are not troubled by suspicions; the good-natured and charitable who rejoice at the good fortune of others, scarcely know what envy means; and he who has realized the Divine within himself recognizes it in all beings, even in the beasts.

And men and women are confirmed in their mental outlook because of the fact that, by the law of cause and effect, they attract to themselves that which they send forth, and so come in contact with people similar to themselves.

The old adage, "Birds of a feather flock together," has a deeper significance than is generally attached to it, for in the thought-world as in the world of matter, each clings to its kind.

Do you wish for kindness? Be kind.
Do you ask for truth? Be true.
What you give of yourself you find;
Your world is a reflex of you.

If you are one of those who are praying for, and looking forward to, a happier world beyond the grave, here is a message of gladness for you, you may enter into and realize that happy world now; it fills the whole universe, and it is within you, waiting for you to find, acknowledge, and possess. Said one who knew the inner laws of Being,"

When men shall say Io here, or Io there, go not after them; the kingdom of God is within you."

What you have to do is to believe this, simply believe it with a mind unshadowed by doubt, and then meditate upon it till you understand it.

You will then begin to purify and to build your inner world, and as you proceed, passing from revelation to revelation, from realization to realization, you will discover the utter powerlessness of outward things beside the magic potency of a self-governed soul.

If thou would'st right the world,
And banish all its evils and its woes,
Make its wild places bloom,
And its drear deserts blossom as the rose,—
Then right thyself.

If thou would'st turn the world

From its long, lone captivity in sin,
Restore all broken hearts,
Slay grief, and let sweet consolation in,—
Turn thou thyself.

If thou would'st cure the world
Of its long sickness, end its grief and pain;
Bring in all-healing joy,
And give to the afflicted rest again,—
Then cure thyself.

If thou would'st wake the world
Out of its dream of death and dark'ning strife,
Bring it to Love and Peace,
And Light and brightness of immortal Life,—
Wake thou thyself.

The Way out of Undesirable Conditions

Having seen and realized that evil is but a passing shadow thrown, by the intercepting self, across the transcendent Form of the Eternal Good, and that the world is a mirror in which each sees a reflection of himself, we now ascend, by firm and easy steps, to that plane of perception whereon is seen and realized the Vision of the Law.

With this realization comes the knowledge that everything is included in a ceaseless interaction of cause and effect, and that nothing can possibly be divorced from law.

From the most trivial thought, word, or act of man, up to the groupings of the celestial bodies, law reigns supreme. No arbitrary condition can, even for one moment, exist, for such a condition would be a denial and an annihilation of law.

Every condition of life is, therefore, bound up in an orderly and harmonious sequence, and the secret and cause of every condition is contained within itself, The law, "Whatsoever a man sows that shall he also reap," is inscribed in flaming letters upon the portal of Eternity, and none can deny it, none can cheat it, none can escape it.

He who puts his hand in the fire must suffer the burning until such time as it has worked itself out, and neither curses nor prayers can avail to alter it.

And precisely the same law governs the realm of mind. Hatred, anger, jealousy, envy, lust, covetousness, all these are fires which bum, and whoever even so much as touches them must suffer the torments of burning.

All these conditions of mind are rightly called "evil," for they are the efforts of the soul to subvert, in its ignorance, the law, an they, therefore, lead to chaos and confusion within, and are sooner or later actualized in the outward circumstances as disease, failure, and misfortune, coupled with grief, pain, and despair.

Whereas love, gentleness, good-will, purity, are cooling airs which breathe peace upon the soul that woes them, and, being in harmony with the Eternal

Law, they become actualized in the form of health, peaceful surroundings, and undeviating success and good fortune.

A thorough understanding of this Great Law which permeates the universe leads to the acquirement of that state of mind known as obedience.

To know that justice, harmony, and love are supreme in the universe is likewise to know that all adverse and painful conditions are the result of our own disobedience to that Law.

Such knowledge leads to strength and power, and it is upon such knowledge alone that a true life and an enduring success and happiness can be built.

To be patient under all circumstances, and to accept all conditions as necessary factors in your training, is to rise superior to all painful conditions, and to overcome them with an overcoming which is sure, and which leaves no fear of their return, for by the power of obedience to law they are utterly slain.

Such an obedient one is working in harmony with the law, has in fact, identified himself with the law, and whatsoever he conquers he conquers for ever, whatsoever he builds can never be destroyed.

The cause of all power, as of all weakness, is within; the secret of all happiness as of all misery is likewise within.

There is no progress apart from unfoldment within, and no sure foothold of prosperity or peace except by orderly advancement in knowledge.

You say you are chained by circumstances; you cry out for better opportunities, for a wider scope, for improved physical conditions, and perhaps you inwardly curse the fate that binds you hand and foot.

It is for you that I write; it is to you that I speak. Listen, and let my words burn themselves into your heart, for that which I say to you is truth:

You may bring about that improved condition in your outward life which you desire, if you will unswervingly resolve to improve your inner life.

I know this pathway looks barren at its commencement (truth always does, it is only error and delusion which are at first inviting and fascinating,) but if you undertake to walk it; if you perseveringly discipline your mind, eradicating your weaknesses, and allowing your soul-forces and spiritual powers to unfold themselves, you will be astonished at the magical changes which will be brought about in your outward life.

As you proceed, golden opportunities will be strewn across your path, and the power and judgment to properly utilize them will spring up within you. Genial friends will come unbidden to you; sympathetic souls will be drawn to you as the needle is to the magnet; and books and all outward aids that you require will come to you unsought.

Perhaps the chains of poverty hang heavily upon you, and you are friendless and alone, and you long with an intense longing that your load may be lightened; but the load continues, and you seem to be enveloped in an ever-increasing darkness.

Perhaps you complain, you bewail your lot; you blame your birth, your parents, your employer, or the unjust Powers who have bestowed upon you so undeservedly poverty and hardship, and upon another affluence and ease.

Cease your complaining and fretting; none of these things which you blame are the cause of your poverty; the cause is within yourself, and where the cause is, there is the remedy.

The very fact that you are a complainer, shows that you deserve your lot; shows that you lack that faith which is the ground of all effort and progress.

There is no room for a complainer in a universe of law, and worry is soul-suicide. By your very attitude of mind you are strengthening the chains which bind you, and are drawing about you the darkness by which you are enveloped, Alter your outlook upon life, and your outward life will alter.

Build yourself up in the faith and knowledge, and make yourself worthy of better surroundings and wider opportunities. Be sure, first of all, that you are making the best of what you have.

Do not delude yourself into supposing that you can step into greater advantages whilst overlooking smaller ones, for if you could, the advantage would be impermanent and you would quickly fall back again in order to learn the lesson which you had neglected.

As the child at school must master one standard before passing onto the next, so, before you can have that greater good which you so desire, must you faithfully employ that which you already possess.

The parable of the talents is a beautiful story illustrative of this truth, for does it not plainly show that if we misuse, neglect, or degrade that which we possess, be it ever so mean and insignificant, even that little will be taken from us, for, by our conduct we show that we are unworthy of it.

Perhaps you are living in a small cottage, and are surrounded by unhealthy and vicious influences.

You desire a larger and more sanitary residence. Then you must fit yourself for such a residence by first of all making your cottage as far as possible a little paradise. Keep it spotlessly clean. Make it look as pretty and sweet as your limited means will allow. Cook your plain food with all care, and arrange your humble table as tastefully as you possibly can.

If you cannot afford a carpet, let your rooms be carpeted with smiles and welcomes, fastened down with the nails of kind words driven in with the hammer of

patience. Such a carpet will not fade in the sun, and constant use will never wear it away.

By so ennobling your present surroundings you will rise above them, and above the need of them, and at the right time you will pass on into the better house and surroundings which have all along been waiting for you, and which you have fitted yourself to occupy.

Perhaps you desire more time for thought and effort, and feel that your hours of labor are too hard and long. Then see to it that you are utilizing to the fullest possible extent what little spare time you have.

It is useless to desire more time, if you are already wasting what little you have; for you would only grow more indolent and indifferent.

Even poverty and lack of time and leisure are not the evils that you imagine they are, and if they hinder you in your progress, it is because you have clothed them in your own weaknesses, and the evil that you see in them is really in yourself. Endeavor to fully and completely realize that in so far as you shape and mould your mind, you are the maker of your destiny, and as, by the transmuting power of self-discipline you realize this more and more, you will come to see that these so-called evils may be converted into blessings.

You will then utilize your poverty for the cultivation of patience, hope and courage; and your lack of time in the gaining of promptness of action and decision of mind, by seizing the precious moments as they present themselves for your acceptance.

As in the rankest soil the most beautiful flowers are grown, so in the dark soil of poverty the choicest flowers of humanity have developed and bloomed.

Where there are difficulties to cope with, and unsatisfactory conditions to overcome, there virtue most flourishes and manifests its glory.

It may be that you are in the employ of a tyrannous master or mistress, and you feel that you are harshly treated. Look upon this also as necessary to your training. Return your employer's unkindness with gentleness and forgiveness.

Practice unceasingly patience and self-control. Turn the disadvantage to account by utilizing it for the gaining of mental and spiritual strength, and by your silent example and influence you will thus be teaching your employer, will be helping him to grow ashamed of his conduct, and will, at the same time, be lifting yourself up to that height of spiritual attainment by which you will be enabled to step into new and more congenial surroundings at the time when they are presented to you.

Do not complain that you are a slave, but lift yourself up, by noble conduct, above the plane of slavery. Before complaining that you are a slave to another, be sure that you are not a slave to self.

Look within; look searchingly, and have no mercy upon yourself. You will find there, perchance, slavish thoughts, slavish desires, and in your daily life and conduct slavish habits.

Conquer these; cease to be a slave to self, and no man will have the power to enslave you. As you overcome self, you will overcome all adverse conditions, and every difficulty will fall before you.

Do not complain that you are oppressed by the rich. Are you sure that if you gained riches you would not be an oppressor yourself?

Remember that there is the Eternal Law which is absolutely just, and that he who oppresses today must himself be oppressed tomorrow; and from this there is no way of escape.

And perhaps you, yesterday (in some former existence) were rich and an oppressor, and that you are now merely paying off the debt which you owe to the Great Law. Practice, therefore, fortitude and faith.

Dwell constantly in mind upon the Eternal justice, the Eternal Good. Endeavor to lift yourself above the personal and the transitory into the impersonal and permanent.

Shake off the delusion that you are being injured or oppressed by another, and try to realize, by a profounder comprehension of your inner life, and the laws which govern that life, that you are only really injured by what is within you. There is no practice more degrading, debasing, and soul-destroying than that of self-pity.

Cast it out from you. While such a canker is feeding upon your heart you can never expect to grow into a fuller life.

Cease from the condemnation of others, and begin to condemn yourself. Condone none of your acts, desires or thoughts that will not bear comparison with spotless purity, or endure the light of sinless good.

By so doing you will be building your house upon the rock of the Eternal, and all that is required for your happiness and well-being will come to you in its own time.

There is positively no way of permanently rising above poverty, or any undesirable condition, except by eradicating those selfish and negative conditions within, of which these are the reflection, and by virtue of which they continue.

The way to true riches is to enrich the soul by the acquisition of virtue. Outside of real heart-virtue there is neither prosperity nor power, but only the appearances of these. I am aware that men make money who have acquired no measure of virtue, and have little desire to do so; but such money does not constitute true riches, and its possession is transitory and feverish.

Here is David's testimony:— For I was envious at the foolish when I saw the prosperity of the wicked...... Their eyes stand out with fatness; they have more than heart could wish. —Verily I have cleansed my heart in vain, and washed my hands in innocence... When I thought to know this it was too painful for me; until I went into the sanctuary of God, then understood I their end."

The prosperity of the wicked was a great trial to David until he went into the sanctuary of God, and then he knew their end.

You likewise may go into that sanctuary. It is within you. It is that state of consciousness which remains when all that is sordid, and personal, and impermanent is risen above, and universal and eternal principles are realized.

That is the God state of consciousness; it is the sanctuary of the Most High. When by long strife and self-discipline, you have succeeded in entering the door of that holy Temple, you will perceive, with unobstructed vision, the end and fruit of all human thought and endeavor, both good and evil.

You will then no longer relax your faith when you see the immoral man accumulating outward riches, for you will know, that he must come again to poverty and degradation.

The rich man who is barren of virtue is, in reality, poor, and as surely, as the waters of the river are drifting to the ocean, so surely is he, in the midst of all his riches, drifting towards poverty and misfortune; and though he die rich, yet must he return to reap the bitter fruit of all of his immorality.

And though he become rich many times, yet as many times must he be thrown back into poverty, until, by long experience and suffering he conquers the poverty within.

But the man who is outwardly poor, yet rich in virtue, is truly rich, and, in the midst of all his poverty he is surely traveling towards prosperity; and abounding joy and bliss await his coming. If you would become truly and permanently prosperous, you must first become virtuous.

It is therefore unwise to aim directly at prosperity, to make it the one object of life, to reach out greedily for it, To do this is to ultimately defeat yourself.

But rather aim at self-perfection, make useful and unselfish service the object of your life, and ever reach out hands of faith towards the supreme and unalterable Good.

You say you desire wealth, not for your own sake, but in order to do good with it, and to bless others. If this is your real motive in desiring wealth, then wealth will come to you; for you are strong and unselfish indeed if, in the midst of riches, you are willing to look upon yourself as steward and not as owner.

But examine well your motive, for in the majority of instances where money is desired for the admitted object of blessing others, the real underlying motive is a love of popularity, and a desire to pose as a philanthropist or reformer.

If you are not doing good with what little you have, depend upon it the more money you got the more selfish you would become, and all the good you appeared to do with your money, if you attempted to do any, would be so much insinuating self-laudation.

If your real desire is to do good, there is no need to wait for money before you do it; you can do it now, this very moment, and just where you are. If you are really so unselfish as you believe yourself to be, you will show it by sacrificing yourself for others now.

No matter how poor you are, there is room for self-sacrifice, for did not the widow put her all into the treasury?

The heart that truly desires to do good does not wait for money before doing it, but comes to the altar of sacrifice and, leaving there the unworthy elements of self, goes out and breathes upon neighbor and stranger, friend and enemy alike the breath of blessedness.

As the effect is related to the cause, so is prosperity and power related to the inward good and poverty and weakness to the inward evil.

Money does not constitute true wealth, nor position, nor power, and to rely upon it alone is to stand upon a slippery place.

Your true wealth is your stock of virtue, and your true power the uses to which you put it. Rectify your heart, and you will rectify your life. Lust, hatred, anger, vanity, pride, covetousness, self-indulgence, self-seeking, obstinacy,— all these are poverty and weakness; whereas love, purity, gentleness, meekness, compassion, generosity, self-forgetfulness, and self-renunciation,— all these are wealth and power.

As the elements of poverty and weakness are overcome, an irresistible and allconquering power is evolved from within, and he who succeeds in establishing himself in the highest virtue, brings the whole world to his feet.

But the rich, as well as the poor, have their undesirable conditions, and are frequently farther removed from happiness than the poor. And here we see how happiness depends, not upon outward aids or possessions, but upon the inward life.

Perhaps you are an employer, and you have endless trouble with those whom you employ, and when you do get good and faithful servants they quickly leave you. As a result you are beginning to lose, or have completely lost, your faith in human nature.

You try to remedy matters by giving better wages, and by allowing certain liberties, yet matters remain unaltered. Let me advise you.

The secret of all your trouble is not in your servants, it is in yourself; and if you look within, with a humble and sincere desire to discover and eradicate your error, you will, sooner or later, find the origin of all your unhappiness.

It may be some selfish desire, or lurking suspicion, or unkind attitude of mind which sends out its poison upon those about you, and reacts upon yourself, even though you may not show it in your manner or speech.

Think of your servants with kindness, consider of them that extremity of service which you yourself would not care to perform were you in their place.

Rare and beautiful is that humility of soul by which a servant entirely forgets himself in his master's good; but far rarer, and beautiful with a divine beauty, is that nobility of soul by which a man, forgetting his own happiness, seeks the happiness of those who are under his authority, and who depend upon him for their bodily sustenance.

And such a man's happiness is increased tenfold, nor does he need to complain of those whom he employs. Said a well known and extensive employer of labor, who never needs to dismiss an employee: "I have always had the happiest relations with my workpeople.

If you ask me how it is to be accounted for, I can only say that it has been my aim from the first to do to them as I would wish to be done by." Herein lies the secret by which all desirable conditions are secured, and all that are undesirable are overcome.

Do you say that you are lonely and unloved, and have "not a friend in the world"? Then, I pray you, for the sake of your own happiness, blame nobody but yourself.

Be friendly towards others, and friends will soon flock round you. Make yourself pure and lovable, and you will be loved by all.

Whatever conditions are rendering your life burdensome, you may pass out of and beyond them by developing and utilizing within you the transforming power of self-purification and self-conquest.

Be it the poverty which galls (and remember that the poverty upon which I have been dilating is that poverty which is a source of misery, and not that voluntary poverty which is the glory of emancipated souls), or the riches which burden, or the many misfortunes, griefs, and annoyances which form the dark background in the web of life, you may overcome them by overcoming the selfish elements within which give them life.

It matters not that by the unfailing Law, there are past thoughts and acts to work out and to atone for, as, by the same law, we are setting in motion, during every moment of our life, fresh thoughts and acts, and we have the power to make them good or ill.

Nor does it follow that if a man (reaping what he has sown) must lose money or forfeit position, that he must also lose his fortitude or forfeit his uprightness, and it is in these that his wealth and power and happiness are to be found. He who clings to self is his own enemy and is surrounded by enemies.

He who relinquishes self is his own savior, and is surrounded by friends like a protecting belt. Before the divine radiance of a pure heart all darkness vanishes and all clouds melt away, and he who has conquered self has conquered the universe.

Come, then, out of your poverty; come out of your pain; come out of your troubles, and sighings, and complainings, and heartaches, and loneliness by coming out of yourself.

Let the old tattered garment of your petty selfishness fall from you, and put on the new garment of universal Love. You will then realize the inward heaven, and it will be reflected in all your outward life.

He who sets his foot firmly upon the path of self-conquest, who walks, aided by the staff of Faith, the highway of self-sacrifice, will assuredly achieve the highest prosperity, and will reap abounding and enduring joy and bliss.

To them that seek the highest good
All things subserve the wisest ends;
Nought comes as ill, and wisdom lends
Wings to all shapes of evil brood.

The dark'ning sorrow veils a Star
That waits to shine with gladsome light;
Hell waits on heaven; and after night
Comes golden glory from afar.

Defeats are steps by which we climb
With purer aim to nobler ends;

Loss leads to gain, and joy attends
True footsteps up the hills of time.

Pain leads to paths of holy bliss,
To thoughts and words and deeds divine—
And clouds that gloom and rays that shine,
Along life's upward highway kiss.

Misfortune does but cloud the way
Whose end and summit in the sky
Of bright success, sunkiss'd and high,
Awaits our seeking and our stay.

The heavy pall of doubts and fears
That clouds the Valley of our hopes,
The shades with which the spirit copes,
The bitter harvesting of tears,

The heartaches, miseries, and griefs,
The bruisings born of broken ties,
All these are steps by which we rise
To living ways of sound beliefs.

Love, pitying, watchful, runs to meet
The Pilgrim from the Land of Fate;
All glory and all good await
The coming of obedient feet.

The Silent Power of Thought: Controlling and Directing One's Forces

The most powerful forces in the universe are the silent forces; and in accordance with the intensity of its power does a force become beneficent when rightly directed, and destructive when wrongly employed.

This is a common knowledge in regard to the mechanical forces, such as steam, electricity, etc., but few have yet learned to apply this knowledge to the realm of mind, where the thought-forces (most powerful of all) are continually being generated and sent forth as currents of salvation or destruction.

At this stage of his evolution, man has entered into the possession of these forces, and the whole trend of his present advancement is their complete subjugation. All the wisdom possible to man on this material earth is to be found only in complete self-mastery, and the command, "Love your enemies," resolves itself into an exhortation to enter here and now, into the possession of that sublime wisdom by taking hold of, mastering and transmuting, those mind forces to which man is now slavishly subject, and by which he is helplessly borne, like a straw on the stream, upon the currents of selfishness.

The Hebrew prophets, with their perfect knowledge of the Supreme Law, always related outward events to inward thought, and associated national disaster or success with the thoughts and desires that dominated the nation at the time.

The knowledge of the causal power of thought is the basis of all their prophecies, as it is the basis of all real wisdom and power. National events are simply the working out of the psychic forces of the nation.

Wars, plagues, and famines are the meeting and clashing of wrongly-directed thought-forces, the culminating points at which destruction steps in as the agent of the Law.

It is foolish to ascribe war to the influence of one man, or to one body of men. It is the crowning horror of national selfishness. It is the silent and conquering thought-forces which bring all things into manifestation.

The universe grew out of thought. Matter in its last analysis is found to be merely objectivized thought. All men's accomplishments were first wrought out in thought, and then objectivized.

The author, the inventor, the architect, first builds up his work in thought, and having perfected it in all its parts as a complete and harmonious whole upon the thought-plane. he then commences to materialize it, to bring it down to the material or sense-plane.

When the thought-forces are directed in harmony with the over-ruling Law, they are up-building and preservative, but when subverted they become disintegrating and self-destructive.

To adjust all your thoughts to a perfect and unswerving faith in the omnipotence and supremacy of Good, is to co-operate with that Good, and to realize within yourself the solution and destruction of all evil. Believe and ye shall live.

And here we have the true meaning of salvation; salvation from the darkness and negation of evil, by entering into, and realizing the living light of the Eternal Good.

Where there is fear, worry, anxiety, doubt, trouble, chagrin, or disappointment, there is ignorance and lack of faith.

All these conditions of mind are the direct outcome of selfishness, and are based upon an inherent belief in the power and supremacy of evil; they therefore constitute practical atheism; and to live in, and become subject to, these negative and soul-destroying conditions of mind is the only real atheism.

It is salvation from such conditions that the race needs, and let no man boast of salvation whilst he is their helpless and obedient slave.

To fear or to worry is as sinful as to curse, for how can one fear or worry if he intrinsically believes in the Eternal justice, the Omnipotent Good, the Boundless Love? To fear, to worry, to doubt, is to deny, to dis-believe.

It is from such states of mind that all weakness and failure proceed, for they represent the annulling and disintegrating of the positive thought-forces which would otherwise speed to their object with power, and bring about their own beneficent results.

To overcome these negative conditions is to enter into a life of power, is to cease to be a slave, and to become a master, and there is only one way by which they can be overcome, and that is by steady and persistent growth in inward knowledge.

To mentally deny evil is not sufficient; it must, by daily practice, be risen above and understood. To mentally affirm the good is inadequate; it must, by unswerving endeavor, be entered into and comprehended.

The intelligent practice of self-control, quickly leads to a knowledge of one's interior thought-forces, and, later on, to the acquisition of that power by which they are rightly employed and directed.

In the measure that you master self, that you control your mental forces instead of being controlled by them, in just such measure will you master affairs and outward circumstances.

Show me a man under whose touch everything crumbles away, and who cannot retain success even when it is placed in his hands, and I will show you a man who dwells continually in those conditions of mind which are the very negation of power.

To be for ever wallowing in the bogs of doubt, to be drawn continually into the quicksands of fear, or blown ceaselessly about by the winds of anxiety, is to be a slave, and to live the life of a slave, even though success and influence be for ever knocking at your door seeking for admittance.

Such a man, being without faith and without self-government, is incapable of the right government of his affairs, and is a slave to circumstances; in reality a slave to himself. Such are taught by affliction, and ultimately pass from weakness to strength by the stress of bitter experience. Faith and purpose constitute the motive-power of life.

There is nothing that a strong faith and an unflinching purpose may not accomplish. By the daily exercise of silent faith, the thought-forces are gathered together, and by the daily strengthening of silent purpose, those forces are directed toward the object of accomplishment.

Whatever your position in life may be, before you can hope to enter into any measure of success, usefulness, and power, you must learn how to focus your thought-forces by cultivating calmness and repose. It may be that you are a business man, and you are suddenly confronted with some overwhelming difficulty or probable disaster. You grow fearful and anxious, and are at your wit's end.

To persist in such a state of mind would be fatal, for when anxiety steps in, correct judgment passes out. Now if you will take advantage of a quiet hour or two in the early morning or at night, and go away to some solitary spot, or to some room in your house where you know you will be absolutely free from intrusion, and, having seated yourself in an easy attitude, you forcibly direct your mind right away from the object of anxiety by dwelling upon something in your life that is pleasing and blissgiving, a calm, reposeful strength will gradually steal into your mind, and your anxiety will pass away.

Upon the instant that you find your mind reverting to the lower plane of worry bring it back again, and re-establish it on the plane of peace and strength.

When this is fully accomplished, you may then concentrate your whole mind upon the solution of your difficulty, and what was intricate and insurmountable to you in your hour of anxiety will be made plain and easy, and you will see, with that clear vision and perfect judgment which belong only to a calm and untroubled mind, the right course to pursue and the proper end to be brought about.

It may be that you will have to try day after day before you will be able to perfectly calm your mind, but if you persevere you will certainly accomplish it. And the course which is presented to you in that hour of calmness must be carried out.

Doubtless when you are again involved in the business of the day, and worries again creep in and begin to dominate you, you will begin to think that the course is a wrong or foolish one, but do not heed such suggestions.

Be guided absolutely and entirely by the vision of calmness, and not by the shadows of anxiety. The hour of calmness is the hour of illumination and correct judgment.

By such a course of mental discipline the scattered thought-forces are re-united, and directed, like the rays of the search-light, upon the problem at issue, with the result that it gives way before them.

There is no difficulty, however great, but will yield before a calm and powerful concentration of thought, and no legitimate object but may be speedily actualized by the intelligent use and direction of one's soul-forces.

Not until you have gone deeply and searchingly into your inner nature, and have overcome many enemies that lurk there, can you have any approximate conception of the subtle power of thought, of its inseparable relation to outward and material things, or of its magical potency, when rightly poised and directed, in readjusting and transforming the life-conditions.

Every thought you think is a force sent out, and in accordance with its nature and intensity will it go out to seek a lodgment in minds receptive to it, and will react upon yourself for good or evil. There is ceaseless reciprocity between mind and mind, and a continual interchange of thought-forces.

Selfish and disturbing thoughts are so many malignant and destructive forces, messengers of evil, sent out to stimulate and augment the evil in other minds, which in turn send them back upon you with added power.

While thoughts that are calm, pure, and unselfish are so many angelic messengers sent out into the world with health, healing, and blessedness upon their wings, counteracting the evil forces; pouring the oil of joy upon the troubled waters of anxiety and sorrow, and restoring to broken hearts their heritage of immortality.

Think good thoughts, and they will quickly become actualized in your outward life in the form of good conditions. Control your soul-forces, and you will be able to shape your outward life as you will.

The difference between a savior and a sinner is this, that the one has a perfect control of all the forces within him; the other is dominated and controlled by them.

There is absolutely no other way to true power and abiding peace, but by self-control, self-government, self-purification. To be at the mercy of your disposition is to be impotent, unhappy, and of little real use in the world.

The conquest of your petty likes and dislikes, your capricious loves and hates, your fits of anger, suspicion, jealousy, and all the changing moods to which you are more or less helplessly subject, this is the task you have before you if you would weave into the web of life the golden threads of happiness and prosperity.

In so far as you are enslaved by the changing moods within you, will you need to depend upon others and upon outward aids as you walk through life.

If you would walk firmly and securely, and would accomplish any achievement, you must learn to rise above and control all such disturbing and retarding vibrations.

You must daily practice the habit of putting your mind at rest, "going into the silence," as it is commonly called. This is a method of replacing a troubled thought with one of peace, a thought of weakness with one of strength.

Until you succeed in doing this you cannot hope to direct your mental forces upon the problems and pursuits of life with any appreciable measure of success. It is a process of diverting one's scattered forces into one powerful channel.

Just as a useless marsh may be converted into a field of golden corn or a fruitful garden by draining and directing the scattered and harmful streams into one wellcut channel, so, he who acquires calmness, and subdues and directs the thoughtcurrents within himself, saves his soul, and fructifies his heart and life.

As you succeed in gaining mastery over your impulses and thoughts you will begin to feel, growing up within you, a new and silent power, and a settled feeling of composure and strength will remain with you.

Your latent powers will begin to unfold themselves, and whereas formerly your efforts were weak and ineffectual, you will now be able to work with that calm confidence which commands success.

And along with this new power and strength, there will be awakened within you that interior Illumination known as "intuition," and you will walk no longer in darkness and speculation, but in light and certainty.

With the development of this soul-vision, judgment and mental penetration will be incalculably increased, and there will evolve within you that prophetic vision by the aid of which you will be able to sense coming events, and to forecast, with remarkable accuracy, the result of your efforts.

And in just the measure that you alter from within will your outlook upon life alter; and as you alter your mental attitude towards others they will alter in their attitude and conduct toward you.

As you rise above the lower, debilitating, and destructive thought-forces, you will come in contact with the positive, strengthening, and up-building currents generated by strong, pure, and noble minds, your happiness will be immeasurably intensified, and you will begin to realize the joy, strength, and power, which are born only of self-mastery.

And this joy, strength, and power will be continually radiating from you, and without any effort on your part, nay, though you are utterly unconscious of it, strong people will be drawn toward you, influence will be put into your hands, and in accordance with your altered thought-world will outward events shape themselves.

"A man's foes are they of his own household," and he who would be useful, strong, and happy, must cease to be a passive receptacle for the negative, beggarly, and impure streams of thought; and as a wise householder commands his servants and invites his guests, so must he learn to command his desires, and to say, with authority, what thoughts he shall admit into the mansion of his soul.

Even a very partial success in self-mastery adds greatly to one's power, and he who succeeds in perfecting this divine accomplishment, enters into possession of undreamed-of wisdom and inward strength and peace, and realizes that all the forces of the universe aid and protect his footsteps who is master of his soul.

Would you scale the highest heaven,

Would you pierce the lowest hell,
Live in dreams of constant beauty,
Or in basest thinkings dwell.

For your thoughts are heaven above you,
And your thoughts are hell below,
Bliss is not, except in thinking,
Torment nought but thought can know.

Worlds would vanish but for thinking;
Glory is not but in dreams;
And the Drama of the ages
From the Thought Eternal streams.

Dignity and shame and sorrow,
Pain and anguish, love and hate
Are but maskings of the mighty
Pulsing Thought that governs Fate.

As the colors of the rainbow
Makes the one uncolored beam,
So the universal changes
Make the One Eternal Dream.

And the Dream is all within you,
And the Dreamer waiteth long
For the Morning to awake him
To the living thought and strong.

That shall make the ideal real,
Make to vanish dreams of hell
In the highest, holiest heaven
Where the pure and perfect dwell.

Evil is the thought that thinks it;
Good, the thought that makes it so
Light and darkness, sin and pureness
Likewise out of thinking grow.

Dwell in thought upon the Grandest,
And the Grandest you shall see ;
Fix your mind upon the Highest,
And the Highest you shall be.

The Secret of Health, Success and Power

We all remember with what intense delight, as children, we listened to the nevertiring fairy-tale. How eagerly we followed the fluctuating fortunes of the good boy or girl, ever protected, in the hour of crisis, from the evil machinations of the scheming witch, the cruel giant, or the wicked king.

And our little hearts never faltered for the fate of the hero or heroine, nor did we doubt their ultimate triumph over all their enemies, for we knew that the fairies were infallible, and that they would never desert those who had consecrated themselves to the good and the true.

And what unspeakable joy pulsated within us when the Fairy-Queen, bringing all her magic to bear at the critical moment, scattered all the darkness and trouble, and granted them the complete satisfaction of all their hopes, and they were "happy ever after."

With the accumulating years, and an ever-increasing intimacy with the so-called "realities" of life, our beautiful fairy-world became obliterated, and its wonderful inhabitants were relegated, in the archives of memory, to the shadowy and unreal.

And we thought we were wise and strong in thus leaving for ever the land of childish dreams, but as we re-become little children in the wondrous world of wisdom, we shall return again to the inspiring dreams of childhood and find that they are, after all, realities.

The fairy-folk, so small and nearly always invisible, yet possessed of an all-conquering and magical power, who bestow upon the good, health, wealth, and happiness, along with all the gifts of nature in lavish profusion, start again into reality and become immortalized in the soul-realm of him who, by growth in wisdom, has entered into a knowledge of the power of thought, and the laws which govern the inner world of being.

To him the fairies live again as thought-people, thought-messengers, thoughtpowers working in harmony with the over-ruling Good. And they who, day by day, endeavor to harmonize their hearts with the heart of the Supreme Good, do in reality acquire true health, wealth, and happiness.

There is no protection to compare with goodness, and by "goodness" I do not mean a mere outward conformity to the rules of morality; I mean pure thought, noble aspiration, unselfish love, and freedom from vainglory.

To dwell continually in good thoughts, is to throw around oneself a psychic atmosphere of sweetness and power which leaves its impress upon all who come in contact with it.

As the rising sun puts to rout the helpless shadows, so are all the impotent forces of evil put to flight by the searching rays of positive thought which shine forth from a heart made strong in purity and faith.

Where there is sterling faith and uncompromising purity there is health, there is success, there is power. In such a one, disease, failure, and disaster can find no lodgment, for there is nothing on which they can feed.

Even physical conditions are largely determined by mental states, and to this truth the scientific world is rapidly being drawn.

The old, materialistic belief that a man is what his body makes him, is rapidly passing away, and is being replaced by the inspiring belief that man is superior to his body, and that his body is what he makes it by the power of thought.

Men everywhere are ceasing to believe that a man is despairing because he is dyspeptic, and are coming to understand that he is dyspeptic because he is despairing, and in the near future, the fact that all disease has its origin in the mind will become common knowledge.

There is no evil in the universe but has its root and origin in the mind, and sin, sickness, sorrow, and affliction do not, in reality, belong to the universal order, are not inherent in the nature of things, but are the direct outcome of our ignorance of the right relations of things.

According to tradition, there once lived, in India, a school of philosophers who led a life of such absolute purity and simplicity that they commonly reached the age of one hundred and fifty years, and to fall sick was looked upon by them as an unpardonable disgrace, for it was considered to indicate a violation of law.

The sooner we realize and acknowledge that sickness, far from being the arbitrary visitation of an offended God, or the test of an unwise Providence, is the result of our own error or sin, the sooner shall we enter upon the highway of health.

Disease comes to those who attract it, to those whose minds and bodies are receptive to it, and flees from those whose strong, pure, and positive thought-sphere generates healing and life-giving currents.

If you are given to anger, worry, jealousy, greed, or any other inharmonious state of mind, and expect perfect physical health, you are expecting the impossible, for you are continually sowing the seeds of disease in your mind.

Such conditions of mind are carefully shunned by the wise man, for he knows them to be far more dangerous than a bad drain or an infected house.

If you would be free from all physical aches and pains, and would enjoy perfect physical harmony, then put your mind in order, and harmonize your thoughts. Think joyful thoughts; think loving thoughts; let the elixir of goodwill course through your veins, and you will need no other medicine. Put away your jealousies, your suspicions, your worries, your hatreds, your selfish indulgences, and you will put away your dyspepsia, your biliousness, your nervousness and aching joints.

If you will persist in clinging to these debilitating and demoralizing habits of mind, then do not complain when your body is laid low with sickness. The following story illustrates the close relation that exists between habits of mind and bodily conditions.

A certain man was afflicted with a painful disease, and he tried one physician after another, but all to no purpose. He then visited towns which were famous for their curative waters, and after having bathed in them all, his disease was more painful than ever.

One night he dreamed that a Presence came to him and said, "Brother, hast thou tried all the means of cure?" and he replied, "I have tried all." "Nay," said the Presence, "Come with me, and I will show thee a healing bath which has escaped thy notice."

The afflicted man followed, and the Presence led him to a clear pool of water, and said, "Plunge thyself in this water and thou shalt surely recover," and thereupon vanished.

The man plunged into the water, and on coming out, Io! his disease had left him, and at the same moment he saw written above the pool the word "Renounce." Upon waking, the fall meaning of his dream flashed across his mind, and looking within he discovered that he had, all along, been a victim to a sinful indulgence, and he vowed that he would renounce it for ever.

He carried out his vow, and from that day his affliction began to leave him, and in a short time he was completely restored to health. Many people complain that they have broken down through over-work. In the majority of such cases the breakdown is more frequently the result of foolishly wasted energy.

If you would secure health you must learn to work without friction. To become anxious or excited, or to worry over needless details is to invite a breakdown.

Work, whether of brain or body, is beneficial and health-giving, and the man who can work with a steady and calm persistency, freed from all anxiety and worry, and with his mind utterly oblivious to all but the work he has in hand, will not only accomplish far more than the man who is always hurried and anxious, but he will retain his health, a boon which the other quickly forfeits.

True health and true success go together, for they are inseparably intertwined in the thought-realm. As mental harmony produces bodily health, so it also leads to a harmonious sequence in the actual working out of one's plans.

Order your thoughts and you will order your life. Pour the oil of tranquility upon the turbulent waters of the passions and prejudices, and the tempests of misfortune, howsoever they may threaten, will be powerless to wreck the barque of your soul, as it threads its way across the ocean of life.

And if that barque be piloted by a cheerful and never-failing faith its course will be doubly sure, and many perils will pass it by which would otherwise attack it.

By the power of faith every enduring work is accomplished. Faith in the Supreme; faith in the over-ruling Law; faith in your work, and in your power to accomplish that work, —here is the rock upon which you must build if you would achieve, if you would stand and not fall.

To follow, under all circumstances, the highest promptings within you; to be always true to the divine self; to rely upon the inward Light, the inward Voice, and to pursue your purpose with a fearless and restful heart, believing that the future will yield unto you the meed of every thought and effort; knowing that the laws of the universe can never fail, and that your own will come back to you with mathematical exactitude, this is faith and the living of faith.

By the power of such a faith the dark waters of uncertainty are divided, every mountain of difficulty crumbles away, and the believing soul passes on unharmed.

Strive, O reader! to acquire, above everything, the priceless possession of this dauntless faith, for it is the talisman of happiness, of success, of peace, of power, of all that makes life great and superior to suffering.

Build upon such a faith, and you build upon the Rock of the Eternal, and with the materials of the Eternal, and the structure that you erect will never be dissolved, for it will transcend all the accumulations of material luxuries and riches, the end of which is dust.

Whether you are hurled into the depths of sorrow or lifted upon the heights of joy, ever retain your hold upon this faith, ever return to it as your rock of refuge, and keep your feet firmly planted upon its immortal and immovable base.

Centered in such a faith, you will become possessed of such a spiritual strength as will shatter, like so many toys of glass, all the forces of evil that are hurled against you, and you will achieve a success such as the mere striver after worldly gain can never know or even dream of. "If ye have faith, and doubt not, ye shall not only do this, ... but if ye shall say unto this mountain, be thou removed and be thou cast into the sea, it shall be done."

There are those today, men and women tabernacled in flesh and blood, who have realized this faith, who live in it and by it day by day, and who, having put it to the uttermost test, have entered into the possession of its glory and peace.

Such have sent out the word of command, and the mountains of sorrow and disappointment, of mental weariness and physical pain have passed from them, and have been cast into the sea of oblivion.

If you will become possessed of this faith you will not need to trouble about your success or failure, and success will come.

You will not need to become anxious about results, but will work joyfully and peacefully, knowing that right thoughts and right efforts will inevitably bring about right results.

I know a lady who has entered into many blissful satisfactions, and recently a friend remarked to her, "Oh, how fortunate you are! You only have to wish for a thing, and it comes to you."

And it did, indeed, appear so on the surface; but in reality all the blessedness that has entered into this woman's life is the direct outcome of the inward state of blessedness which she has, throughout life, been cultivating and training toward perfection.

Mere wishing brings nothing but disappointment; it is living that tells.

The foolish wish and grumble; the wise, work and wait. And this woman had worked; worked without and within, but especially within upon heart and soul; and with the invisible hands of the spirit she had built up, with the precious stones of faith, hope, joy, devotion, and love, a fair temple of light, whose glorifying radiance was ever round about her.

It beamed in her eye; it shone through her countenance; it vibrated in her voice; and all who came into her presence felt its captivating spell.

And as with her, so with you. Your success, your failure, your influence, your whole life you carry about with you, for your dominant trends of thought are the determining factors in your destiny.

Send forth loving, stainless, and happy thoughts, and blessings will fall into your hands, and your table will be spread with the cloth of peace.

Send forth hateful, impure, and unhappy thoughts, and curses will rain down upon you, and fear and unrest will wait upon your pillow. You are the unconditional maker of your fate, be that fate what it may. Every moment you are sending forth from you the influences which will make or mar your life.

Let your heart grow large and loving and unselfish, and great and lasting will be your influence and success, even though you make little money.

Confine it within the narrow limits of self-interest, and even though you become a millionaire your influence and success, at the final reckoning will be found to be utterly insignificant. Cultivate, then, this pure and unselfish spirit, and combine with purity and faith, singleness of purpose, and you are evolving from within the elements, not only of abounding health and enduring success, but of greatness and power.

If your present position is distasteful to you, and your heart is not in your work, nevertheless perform your duties with scrupulous diligence, and whilst resting your mind in the idea that the better position and greater opportunities are waiting for you, ever keep an active mental outlook for budding possibilities, so that when the critical moment arrives, and the new channel presents itself, you will step into it with your mind fully prepared for the undertaking, and with that intelligence and foresight which is born of mental discipline.

Whatever your task may be, concentrate your whole mind upon it, throw into it all the energy of which you are capable. The faultless completion of small tasks leads inevitably to larger tasks. See to it that you rise by steady climbing, and you will never fall. And herein lies the secret of true power.

Learn, by constant practice, how to husband your resources, and to concentrate them, at any moment, upon a given point. The foolish waste all their mental and spiritual energy in frivolity, foolish chatter, or selfish argument, not to mention wasteful physical excesses.

If you would acquire overcoming power you must cultivate poise and passivity. You must be able to stand alone. All power is associated with immovability. The mountain, the massive rock, the storm-tried oak, all speak to us of power, because of their combined solitary grandeur and defiant fixity;

while the shifting sand, the yielding twig, and the waving reed speak to us of weakness, because they are movable and non-resistant, and are utterly useless when detached from their fellows.

He is the man of power who, when all his fellows are swayed by some emotion or passion, remains calm and unmoved. He only is fitted to command and control who has succeeded in commanding and controlling himself.

The hysterical, the fearful, the thoughtless and frivolous, let such seek company, or they will fall for lack of support; but the calm, the fearless, the thoughtful, and let such seek the solitude of the forest, the desert, and the mountain-top, and to their power more power will be added, and they will more and more successfully stem the psychic currents and whirlpools which engulf mankind.

Passion is not power; it is the abuse of power, the dispersion of power. Passion is like a furious storm which beats fiercely and wildly upon the embattled rock whilst power is like the rock itself, which remains silent and unmoved through it all.

That was a manifestation of true power when Martin Luther, wearied with the persuasions of his fearful friends, who were doubtful as to his safety should he go to Worms, replied, "If there were as many devils in Worms as there are tiles on the housetops I would go."

And when Benjamin Disraeli broke down in his first Parliamentary speech, and brought upon himself the derision of the House, that was an exhibition of germinal power when he exclaimed, "The day will come when you will consider it an honor to listen to me."

When that young man, whom I knew, passing through continual reverses and misfortunes, was mocked by his friends and told to desist from further effort, and he replied, "The time is not far distant when you will marvel at my good fortune and success," he showed that he was possessed of that silent and irresistible power which has taken him over innumerable difficulties, and crowned his life with success.

If you have not this power, you may acquire it by practice, and the beginning of power is likewise the beginning of wisdom. You must commence by overcoming those purposeless trivialities to which you have hitherto been a willing victim.

Boisterous and uncontrolled laughter, slander and idle talk, and joking merely to raise a laugh, all these things must be put on one side as so much waste of valuable energy.

St. Paul never showed his wonderful insight into the hidden laws of human progress to greater advantage than when he warned the Ephesians against "Foolish talking and jesting which is not convenient," for to dwell habitually in such practices is to destroy all spiritual power and life.

As you succeed in rendering yourself impervious to such mental dissipations you will begin to understand what true power is, and you will then commence to grapple with the more powerful desires and appetites which hold your soul in bondage, and bar the way to power, and your further progress will then be made clear.

Above all be of single aim; have a legitimate and useful purpose, and devote yourself unreservedly to it. Let nothing draw you aside ; remember that the doubleminded man is unstable in all his ways.

Be eager to learn, but slow to beg. Have a thorough understanding of your work, and let it be your own; and as you proceed, ever following the inward Guide, the infallible Voice, you will pass on from victory to victory, and will rise step by step to higher resting-places, and your ever-broadening outlook will gradually reveal to you the essential beauty and purpose of life.

Self-purified, health will be yours; faith-protected, success will be yours; self-governed, power will be yours, and all that you do will prosper, for, ceasing to be a disjointed unit, self-enslaved, you will be in harmony with the Great Law, working no longer against, but with, the Universal Life, the Eternal Good.

And what health you gain it will remain with you; what success you achieve will be beyond all human computation, and will never pass away; and what influence and power you wield will continue to increase throughout the ages, for it will be a part of that unchangeable Principle which supports the universe.

This, then, is the secret of health —a pure heart and a well-ordered mind ; this is the secret of success —an unfaltering faith, and a wisely-directed purpose; and to rein in, with unfaltering will, the dark steed of desire, this is the secret of power.

All ways are waiting for my feet to tread,
The light and dark, the living and the dead,
The broad and narrow way, the high and low,
The good and bad, and with quick step or slow,
I now may enter any way I will,
And find, by walking, which is good, which ill.

And all good things my wandering feet await,
If I but come, with vow inviolate,
Unto the narrow, high and holy way
Of heart-born purity, and therein stay;
Walking, secure from him who taunts and scorns,
To flowery meads, across the path of thorns.

And I may stand where health, success, and power
Await my coming, if, each fleeting hour,
I cling to love and patience; and abide
With stainlessness; and never step aside
From high integrity ; so shall I see
At last the land of immortality.

And I may seek and find; I may achieve,
I may not claim, but, losing, may retrieve.
The law bends not for me, but I must bend
Unto the law, if I would reach the end
Of my afflictions, if I would restore
My soul to Light and Life, and weep no more.

Not mine the arrogant and selfish claim
To all good things; be mine the lowly aim
To seek and find, to know and comprehend,
And wisdom-ward all holy footsteps wend,
Nothing is mine to claim or to command,
But all is mine to know and understand.

The Secret of Abounding Happiness

Great is the thirst for happiness, and equally great is the lack of happiness. The majority of the poor long for riches, believing that their possession would bring them supreme and lasting happiness.

Many who are rich, having gratified every desire and whim, suffer from ennui and repletion, and are farther from the possession of happiness even than the very poor.

If we reflect upon this state of things it will ultimately lead us to a knowledge of the all important truth that happiness is not derived from mere outward possessions, nor misery from the lack of them; for if this were so, we should find the poor always miserable, and the rich always happy, whereas the reverse is frequently the case.

Some of the most wretched people whom I have known were those who were surrounded with riches and luxury, whilst some of the brightest and happiest people I have met were possessed of only the barest necessities of life.

Many men who have accumulated riches have confessed that the selfish gratification which followed the acquisition of riches has robbed life of its sweetness, and that they were never so happy as when they were poor.

What, then, is happiness, and how is it to be secured? Is it a figment, a delusion, and is suffering alone perennial? We shall find, after earnest observation and reflection, that all, except those who have entered the way of wisdom, believe that happiness is only to be obtained by the gratification of desire.

It is this belief, rooted in the soil of ignorance, and continually watered by selfish cravings, that is the cause of all the misery in the world.

And I do not limit the word desire to the grosser animal cravings; it extends to the higher psychic realm, where far more powerful, subtle, and insidious cravings hold in bondage the intellectual and refined, depriving them of all that beauty, harmony, and purity of soul whose expression is happiness.

Most people will admit that selfishness is the cause of all the unhappiness in the world, but they fall under the soul-destroying delusion that it is somebody else's selfishness, and not their own.

When you are willing to admit that all your unhappiness is the result of your own selfishness you will not be far from the gates of Paradise; but so long as you are convinced that it is the selfishness of others that is robbing you of joy, so long will you remain a prisoner in your self-created purgatory.

Happiness is that inward state of perfect satisfaction which is joy and peace, and from which all desire is eliminated. The satisfaction which results from gratified desire is brief and illusionary, and is always followed by an increased demand for gratification.

Desire is as insatiable as the ocean, and clamors louder and louder as its demands are attended to.

It claims ever-increasing service from its deluded devotees, until at last they are struck down with physical or mental anguish, and are hurled into the purifying fires of suffering. Desire is the region of hell, and all torments are centered there.

The giving up of desire is the realization of heaven, and all delights await the pilgrim there,

> I sent my soul through the invisible,
> Some letter of that after life to spell,
> And by-and-by my soul returned to me,
> And whispered, I myself am heaven and hell,"

Heaven and hell are inward states. Sink into self and all its gratifications, and you sink into hell; rise above self into that state of consciousness which is the utter denial and forgetfulness of self, and you enter heaven.

Self is blind, without judgment, not possessed of true knowledge, and always leads to suffering. Correct perception, unbiased judgment, and true knowledge belong only to the divine state, and only in so far as you realize this divine consciousness can you know what real happiness is.

So long as you persist in selfishly seeking for your own personal happiness, so long will happiness elude you, and you will be sowing the seeds of wretchedness.

In so far as you succeed in losing yourself in the service of others, in that measure will happiness come to you, and you will reap a harvest of bliss.

It is in loving, not in being loved,

The heart is blessed;
It is in giving, not in seeking gifts,
We find our quest.

Whatever be thy longing or thy need,
That do thou give;
So shall thy soul be fed, and thou indeed
Shalt truly live.

Cling to self, and you cling to sorrow, relinquish self, and you enter into peace. To seek selfishly is not only to lose happiness, but even that which we believe to be the source of happiness.

See how the glutton is continually looking about for a new delicacy wherewith to stimulate his deadened appetite; and how, bloated, burdened, and diseased, scarcely any food at last is eaten with pleasure.

Whereas, he who has mastered his appetite, and not only does not seek, but never thinks of gustatory pleasure, finds delight in the most frugal meal. The angel-form of happiness, which men, looking through the eyes of self, imagine they see in gratified desire, when clasped is always found to be the skeleton of misery. Truly, "He that seeketh his life shall lose it, and he that loseth his life shall find it."

Abiding happiness will come to you when, ceasing to selfishly cling, you are willing to give up. When you are willing to lose, unreservedly, that impermanent thing which is so dear to you, and which, whether you cling to it or not, will one day be snatched from you, then you will find that that which seemed to you like a painful loss, turns out to be a supreme gain.

To give up in order to gain, than this there is no greater delusion, nor no more prolific source of misery; but to be willing to yield up and to suffer loss, this is indeed the Way of Life.

How is it possible to find real happiness by centering ourselves in those things which, by their very nature, must pass away? Abiding and real happiness can only be found by centering ourselves in that which is permanent.

Rise, therefore, above the clinging to and the craving for impermanent things, and you will then enter into a consciousness of the Eternal, and as, rising above self, and by growing more and more into the spirit of purity, self-sacrifice and universal Love, you become centered in that consciousness, you will realize that happiness which has no reaction, and which can never be taken from you.

The heart that has reached utter self-forgetfulness in its love for others has not only become possessed of the highest happiness but has entered into immortality, for it has realized the Divine.

Look back upon your life, and you will find that the moments of supremest happiness were those in which you uttered some word, or performed some act, of compassion or self-denying love. Spiritually, happiness and harmony are, synonymous.

Harmony is one phase of the Great Law whose spiritual expression is love. All selfishness is discord, and to be selfish is to be out of harmony with the Divine order.

As we realize that all-embracing love which is the negation of self, we put ourselves in harmony with the divine music, the universal song, and that ineffable melody which is true happiness becomes our own.

Men and women are rushing hither and thither in the blind search for happiness, and cannot find it; nor ever will until they recognize that happiness is already within them and round about them, filling the universe, and that they, in their selfish searching are shutting themselves out from it.

I followed happiness to make her mine,
Past towering oak and swinging ivy vine.
She fled, I chased, o'er slanting hill and dale,
O'er fields and meadows, in the purpling vale;
Pursuing rapidly o'er dashing stream.
I scaled the dizzy cliffs where eagles scream;
I traversed swiftly every land and M.
But always happiness eluded me.

Exhausted, fainting, I pursued no more,
But sank to rest upon a barren shore.
One came and asked for food, and one for alms
I placed the bread and gold in bony palms.
One came for sympathy, and one for rest;
I shared with every needy one my best;
When, Io! sweet Happiness, with form divine,
Stood by me, whispering softly, 'I am thine'.

These beautiful lines of Burleigh's express the secret of all abounding happiness. Sacrifice the personal and transient, and you rise at once into the impersonal and permanent.

Give up that narrow cramped self that seeks to render all things subservient to its own petty interests, and you will enter into the company of the angels, into the very heart and essence of universal Love.

Forget yourself entirely in the sorrows of others and in ministering to others, and divine happiness will emancipate you from all sorrow and suffering.

"Taking the first step with a good thought, the second with a good word, and the third with a good deed, I entered Paradise." And you also may enter into Paradise by pursuing the same course. It is not beyond, it is here. It is realized only by the unselfish.

It is known in its fullness only to the pure in heart. If you have not realized this unbounded happiness you may begin to actualize it by ever holding before you the lofty ideal of unselfish love, and aspiring towards it.

Aspiration or prayer is desire turned upward. It is the soul turning toward its Divine source, where alone permanent satisfaction can be found. By aspiration the destructive forces of desire are transmuted into divine and all-preserving energy.

To aspire is to make an effort to shake off the trammels of desire; it is the prodigal made wise by loneliness and suffering, returning to his Father's Mansion.

As you rise above the sordid self; as you break, one after another, the chains that bind you, will you realize the joy of giving, as distinguished from the misery of grasping — giving of your substance; giving of your intellect; giving of the love and light that is growing within you.

You will then understand that it is indeed "more blessed to give than to receive." But the giving must be of the heart without any taint of self, without desire for reward. The gift of pure love is always attended with bliss. If, after you have given, you are wounded because you are not thanked or flattered, or your name put in the paper, know then that your gift was prompted by vanity and not by love, and you were merely giving in order to get; were not really giving, but grasping.

Lose yourself in the welfare of others; forget yourself in all that you do; this is the secret of abounding happiness.

Ever be on the watch to guard against selfishness, and learn faithfully the divine lessons of inward sacrifice; so shall you climb the highest heights of happiness, and shall remain in the neverclouded sunshine of universal joy, clothed in the shining garment of immortality.

Are you searching for the happiness that does not fade away?

Are you looking for the joy that lives, and leaves no grievous day?
Are you panting for the waterbrooks of Love, and Life, and Peace?
Then let all dark desires depart, and selfish seeking cease.
Are you ling'ring in the paths of pain, grief-haunted, stricken sore?
Are you wand'ring in the ways that wound your weary feet the more?
Are you sighing for the Resting-Place where tears and sorrows cease?
Then sacrifice your selfish heart and find the Heart of Peace.

The Realization of Prosperity

It is granted only to the heart that abounds with integrity, trust, generosity and love to realize true prosperity. The heart that is not possessed of these qualities cannot know prosperity, for prosperity, like happiness, is not an outward possession, but an inward realization.

The greedy man may become a millionaire, but he will always be wretched, and mean, and poor, and will even consider himself outwardly poor so long as there is a man in the world who is richer than himself, whilst the upright, the open-handed and loving will realize a full and rich prosperity, even though their outward possessions may be small.

He is poor who is dissatisfied; he is rich who is contented with what he has, and he is richer who is generous with what he has.

When we contemplate the fact that the universe is abounding in all good things, material as well as spiritual, and compare it with man's blind eagerness to secure a few gold coins, or a few acres of dirt, it is then that we realize how dark and ignorant selfishness is; it is then that we know that self-seeking is self-destruction.

Nature gives all, without reservation, and loses nothing; man, grasping all, loses everything.

If you would realize true prosperity do not settle down, as many have done, into the belief that if you do right everything will go wrong. Do not allow the word "competition" to shake your faith in the supremacy of righteousness.

I care not what men may say about the "laws of competition," for do I not know the unchangeable Law, which shall one day put them all to rout, and which puts them to rout even now in the heart and life of the righteous man?

And knowing this Law I can contemplate all dishonesty with undisturbed repose, for I know where certain destruction awaits it. Under all circumstances do that which you believe to be right, and trust the Law; trust the Divine Power that is imminent in the universe, and it will never desert you, and you will always be protected.

By such a trust all your losses will be converted into gains, and all curses which threaten will be transmuted into blessings. Never let go of integrity, generosity, and love, for these, coupled with energy, will lift you into the truly prosperous state.

Do not believe the world when it tells you that you must always attend to "number one" first, and to others afterwards. To do this is not to think of others at all, but only of one's own comforts.

To those who practice this the day will come when they will be deserted by all, and when they cry out in their loneliness and anguish there will be no one to hear and help them. To consider one's self before all others is to cramp and warp and hinder every noble and divine impulse.

Let your soul expand, let your heart reach out to others in loving and generous warmth, and great and lasting will be your joy, and all prosperity will come to you. Those who have wandered from the highway of righteousness guard themselves against competition; those who always pursue the right need not to trouble about such defense.

This is no empty statement, There are men today who, by the power of integrity and faith, have defied all competition, and who, without swerving in the least from their methods, when competed with, have risen steadily into prosperity, whilst those who tried to undermine them have fallen back defeated.

To possess those inward qualities which constitute goodness is to be armored against all the powers of evil, and to be doubly protected in every time of trial; and to build' oneself up in those qualities is to build up a success which cannot be shaken, and to enter into a prosperity which will endure forever.

The White Robe of the Heart Invisible
Is stained with sin and sorrow, grief and pain,
And all repentant pools and springs of prayer
Shall not avail to wash it white again.

While in the path of ignorance I walk,
The stains of error will not cease to cling
Defilements mark the crooked path of self,
Where anguish lurks and disappointments sting.

Knowledge and wisdom only can avail
To purify and make my garment clean,
For therein lie love's waters ; therein rests
Peace undisturbed, eternal, and serene.

Sin and repentance is the path of pain,
Knowledge and wisdom is the path of Peace
By the near way of practice I will find
Where bliss begins, how pains and sorrows cease.

Self shall depart, and Truth shall take its place
The Changeless One, the Indivisible
Shall take up His abode in me, and cleanse
The White Robe of the Heart Invisible.

www.ingramcontent.com/pod-product-compliance
Lightning Source LLC
Chambersburg PA
CBHW051830040426
42447CB00006B/459